T0327908

C D

**A
COOKBOOK BY
ROSA CIENFUEGOS**

THE FOOD OF MEXICO CITY

Smith Street Books

INTRODUCTION 7
THE MEXICAN PANTRY 12

one

DESAYUNOS

BREAKFAST

14

two

ANTOJITOS Y BEBIDAS

SNACKS & DRINKS

38

five

COMIDA CORRIDA

SET MEALS

134

six

MARISCOS

SEAFOOD

164

BASICS 224
FOOD LOVERS' GUIDE 240
ABOUT THE AUTHOR 249
THANK YOU 251
INDEX 252

three

TACOS

TACOS

80

four

SOPAS

SOUPS

112

seven

POSTRES

DESSERTS

184

eight

SALSAS

SALSAS

204

MEXICO CITY MI AMOR

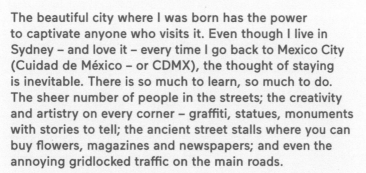

The beautiful city where I was born has the power to captivate anyone who visits it. Even though I live in Sydney – and love it – every time I go back to Mexico City (Cuidad de México – or CDMX), the thought of staying is inevitable. There is so much to learn, so much to do. The sheer number of people in the streets; the creativity and artistry on every corner – graffiti, statues, monuments with stories to tell; the ancient street stalls where you can buy flowers, magazines and newspapers; and even the annoying gridlocked traffic on the main roads.

There are so many dishes and tacos to try, and not enough nights to dance, drink or just to eat an elote on a street corner. I would need an extra stomach to taste everything I want to eat. The street parties, the traditional dances around the suburbs, people coming together just for the sheer pleasure of being there …. Tears run down my face when I leave, and I can only soothe my breaking heart by promising that I'll be back as soon as I can.

My home town is one of the biggest cities in Latin America. Tenochtitlan was founded by the Mexica around 1325 and became the capital of the Aztec Empire. Although it was almost completely destroyed by Spanish colonisation, there are still some Aztec constructions to be seen, such as Templo Mayor near Zócalo. There are many such Aztec buildings buried underneath the Spanish buildings – I wonder at their beauty and suspect that one day they'll emerge again from the ground to shine back at the world!

The city is the place where almost every Mexican dreams to be, dreams to live and dreams to make a living. Mexico City – where alongside the tantalising smell of garnachas and taquitos, wafts the smell of success and opportunities for all. This magical, colourful, vibrant place with its colonial architecture, churches, palaces and castle, through to the suburbs with their modern elegant skyscrapers, gathers traditions from all over the country and has the ability to engage you and make you fall in love.

In the early morning you can enjoy the daily ceremony of the Mexican flag being hoisted up the flagpole right in the middle of Zócalo Square. You'll share the space with hurried people rushing to work, or buying breakfast on the streets. Mexican people rush all the time and life in the city is fast and competitive – after a time in the city, even I feel

frustrated when I travel to the countryside, where life is slow and tranquil! From early morning to after midnight, the city's noise is ever-present. There is music everywhere, the clamour of people, car horns or merchants yelling about what they are selling at the tops of their voices.

Dreams come true for many people in CDMX – not only those from overseas, but also Mexicans from different states and the countryside, who move there in search of a different life. After the conquest of the Aztecs, the first capital of New Spain was Coyoacan in the south of the city. Its name means 'place of the coyotes' and its colonial streets display a startling combination of past and present. It's one of the many places where foreigners from overseas often start their life in the city. You can feel the love and respect they have for the streets, and for the people who came before, bringing their own cultures, indigenous traditions, dances, music, rituals, ingredients and magnificent dishes with them. Within a few years these traditional dishes might become the next must-have 'street food' at stalls, restaurants, fondas and even exclusive restaurants.

In Mexico City you can find dishes from every state, made by proud chefs or cooks who, like me, found their passion through missing what connects us to our heritage and family traditions. That longing empowers us to step up and share that little dish made with that specific ingredient, and with a magic touch of love and nostalgia. So, the state of Puebla is well known for its mole, chiles en nogada and cemitas; Yucatan for its delicious cochinita pibil, panuchos or habanero sauces; Oaxaca its tlayudas, cheese and chocolate; and Jalisco for pozole, birria and, of course, tequila!

There are more than 20 million people living in CDMX, which is also the country's smallest state, and vendors have to be creative to pique the interest of Mexicans throughout the day – everything needs to be either different, cool or new to catch the eye of the chilangos – it's a constant competition!

Each chapter in this book could have had more than 100 recipes – I'm sure there are dishes in the city that I have never tried, seen or even heard of! Food unites us and you can feel and see it at every place. There will always be someone saying 'provecho' – enjoy! – either as you arrive at or leave the table. They don't need to know you, it's just good manners and part of our values.

I'd like to say that Mexicans eat the whole day long! But it is probably only five times a day – breakfast, a snack around midday, lunch at 2–3 pm, another snack about 5–6 pm and dinner at 9–10 pm. Not that the schedule is mandatory, but there will always be a nearby food vendor urging you to try something to eat!

A typical day's eating in the city might include chilaquiles con huevo for breakfast, obviously with a good café de olla; fruit or veggies with salt, lime juice, Tajin seasoning and Botanera sauce for a midday snack; comida corrida for lunch; dorilocos for a late snack; and tacos de tripa for dinner. We also love to have coffee before bed, with a piece of sweet bread or milk, so there will always be dessert too!

The importance of not leaving home to start your day on an empty stomach comes from our ancestors and abuelitas – grandmothers – who understood and lived through hunger during the Mexican Revolution. They will always push you to eat something before leaving home, and they will always be worried about you getting your full meals during the day! Gracias, abuelitas Mexicanas!

Luckily, we also have street breakfast options, if you didn't have time to make something at home. The star option in Mexico City is definitely the guajolota – a tamal inside a bread roll. You can only find this delicacy in the city – it is a delicious, cheap and filling meal that is highly recommended.

Tortillas are on the table every day, freshly made from the local tortilleria from early morning until 5 pm, when lunchtime is truly over. Kilo upon kilo of ground corn is nixtamalised every day, to then create thousands of tortillas to feed a whole country.

I'd like to say you can easily eat whatever taco you like whenever you want it, but the truth is, different tacos are sold at particular times of the day. Tacos de guisado are commonly seen from morning to lunchtime, street-style tacos are enjoyed mainly at night time, carnitas or mixiotes are a midday sort of taco, while barbacoa are a weekend-morning taco ... but I'm not here to judge, so eat them whenever you find them!

A Mexican lunch is usually a larger meal, comprising soup, rice, beans, a main dish and tortillas, and dessert – served as the comida corrida, a sort of 'set meal'. They are cheap and fast and often served in cocinas economicas, small humble restaurants found in the food-court areas of mercados, or near primary schools where the crowds are easy to catch. They are open from early morning to mid-afternoon. Every mercado has its own food-court area, plus stalls where local ingredients are for sale and you can buy juices or fresh brews, seafood, desserts and garnachas.

Cantinas are similar to pubs. The main activity is drinking, but the allure of 'free food' is a drawcard. Some cantinas just keep bringing small plates of food to nibble with drinks; others have a proper menu where you can order pancita, birria, enchiladas, caldo de camaron and much more. They will often have entertainment, such as live music, karaoke or mariachi bands, and customers will spend the day eating, drinking and singing!

I hope to pass on at least a little bit of my love for CDMX through this book. Perhaps not every dish originated in the Mexican capital, but they have now become part of it, and the mix of ingredients brought by immigrants only adds to the boundless creations. I encourage you to experiment, too.

Come and visit our beautiful and dear CDMX. Lose yourself in its lovely craziness and enjoy every second. You will never regret it!

THE
MEXICAN
PANTRY

Most of the following ingredients are proudly 100 per cent Mexican and you'll find many of them in the recipes in this book. The majority can be purchased from Latin American supermarkets or online.

Achiote

Sold in small blocks, this paste made from annatto seeds is often used to give a radiant colour and sour flavour to food. It is one of the signature ingredients of Yucatan cuisine.

Avocados

The avocado was first discovered around 500 BC by the Aztecs who named it āhuacatl, meaning 'testicle', due to the way the fruit hangs on trees. Today, the humble avocado, of which Mexico is still the world's biggest producer, is found in every Mexican home, where it's added to everything from tacos to tortas, dips to salsas, or just scooped with a spoon. Even if your meal doesn't call for avocado, we still often serve a cheeky avocado taco at the start or end of the main meal.

Beans

These dried legumes are a staple in every Mexican household. Generally speaking, pinto beans are more commonly found in Mexico's north, while black beans are used in central and southern Mexican cooking. Beans are used to make Frijoles refritos (see page 227), which is used as a spread or filling for tacos and tortas.

Cacao

Is there anyone who doesn't like chocolate? Perhaps Mexico's most famous export, cacao was worshipped, used as currency and consumed as a bitter drink before the arrival of the Spanish in the 16th century. They took the cocoa bean to Europe where sugar was added to make the much-loved treat we all know and love today (although some Mexicans will argue that Mexican chocolate is still the best). We eat cacao to treat depression, sadness, colds and flu, or use it to make mole or any number of sweet treats.

Chamoy

This versatile condiment, made with fresh or dried apricots, chillies and tangy lime powder, adds a delightful tang to dishes and drinks. It is most commonly served with fruit, fries, chicarrones and even in cocktails. Try making your own chamoy on page 222.

Cheese

Oaxaca cheese (also known as quesillo) is a white semi-hard cheese from, unsurprisingly, Oaxaca. It is one of Mexico's most popular cheeses and it is used in any dish that requires melted cheese. Fresco cheese (or fresh cheese) is commonly used to top garnachas, soups, enchiladas and tostadas. A mild feta is a good alternative. Asadero cheese is a hard cheese similar to haloumi that's popular in the north of Mexico. Requesón is a soft, sour cheese that's also used to top garnachas or tacos. Ricotta is a good substitute.

Chillies

There are more than 150 varieties of chilli in Mexico, along with countless ways to prepare them. Some of the most popular include serrano, jalapeno, chipotle, guajillo, pasilla, ancho and chile de árbol, and you will find these chillies used in many of the recipes in this book in both their fresh and dried forms. Dried chillies are easy to buy in bulk online.

Corn

The foundation of Mexican cuisine, corn is Mexico's most common grain with 59 indigenous varieties to choose from. It forms the basis of tamales, tacos, quesadillas, gorditas, tostadas, desserts and drinks. It is estimated that corn is the main ingredient in more than half of all Mexican dishes, and tortillas are nearly always served with the main meal. In Mexico, white, yellow and blue corn is most commonly ground into flour for tortillas. Huitlacoche (corn smut) is a corn fungus that grows on some corn. It is considered to be a truffle-like delicacy.

Cream

Thickened cream or sour cream are must-have ingredients for topping garnachas, enchiladas and chilaquiles, and for making desserts. I like to add half thickened cream and half sour cream when adding cream to my savoury dishes.

Epazote

This aromatic herb native to Central America is often added to beans, quesadillas, soups and teas. It has a strong, almost medicinal flavour that adds depth to dishes, but it can be an acquired taste to anyone eating it for the first time. Epazote can aid digestion and reduce bloating, although consuming too much can lead to an upset stomach.

Limes

Although not indigenous to Mexico, it's impossible to imagine a Mexican meal without the addition of this ubiquitous citrus. Limes are served with tacos, garnachas, seafood, desserts or in cocktails, where they add a sour tang to dishes, which helps to cut through rich flavours.

Masa

The resulting dough from mixing nixtamalised corn flour (masa harina) and water, masa is used to make tortillas, quesadillas, gorditas, sopes, huaraches and more. Do not confuse nixtamilised corn flour with regular corn meal or flour when buying flour to make your dough.

Nopales

Also known as the prickly pear cactus, nopales are the edible pads of the nopales cactus and are sold fresh and tinned throughout Mexico. They have a mild and slightly sour flavour, as well as being slightly sticky. Sliced and cooked nopales are often added to tacos or served in salads. In Mexico, nopales and the fruit from the cactus are added to juices and smoothies. Outside of Mexico, the tinned variety is readily available.

Onions

As in many cuisines, onions feature heavily in Mexican cooking. White onions, which are sweeter and less astringent than brown onions, are nearly always used. They are often added raw to salsas and salads or used as a garnish.

Tajín

A chilli, lime and salt powder with a sour taste, that's often sprinkled on fruit, vegetables, beer, popcorn, lollies and even soups. It goes with everything!

Tomatillos

Also known as the Mexican husk tomato, despite their name tomatillos are not related to tomatoes. The fruit has a tangy, sour taste and can be eaten cooked or raw.

Valentina sauce

This famous Mexican condiment is a staple in kitchens throughout Mexico. It combines cayenne chillies, vinegar and salt to produce a hot sauce that's drizzled on nearly everything. Valentina sauce comes in two varieties – hot and extra hot. You can replace it with Buffalo, Tapatio or Botanera hot sauces, but Valentina sauce is the most traditional.

DESAYUNOS

DESAYUNOS

DESAYUNOS

THE
STOMACH
ALWAYS

'La panza
es primero.'

COMES
FIRST!

My grandma would always say, 'Mija, don't leave the house without eating'. A good, healthy and fulfilling breakfast is the most important meal of the day, so Abuelita would chase me, my brother and sister around the kitchen to have us eat at least a little of the range of delicious bites she'd whip up every morning.

Thank you, Abuelita, for passing on your knowledge, generation after generation. Today my mum repeats that phrase over and over, and I might get to the same point with my son pretty soon. Mexican families all tend to love and respect their abuelitas. Grandmas are a huge part of our family, education, tradition and values system – so we listen to them and eat when they tell us to!

So, what is a Mexican breakfast? It could be as simple as a tamal or a sweet bread with coffee. Huevos (eggs) are very traditional, and we have many, many combinations! You might not find them at street stalls, but every mercado will sell egg dishes in the early morning, along with black coffee and freshly made tortillas.

Mexico City wakes before sunrise and, if you're up then, you'll find all the biggest mercados open and busy. They're in charge of selling fresh ingredients for all the city's food stalls, who, in turn, are rushing to have everything ready for preparing tacos, atole, coffee, sweet bread, chilaquiles, tortas, garnachas and – our favourite 'chilango' breakfast – tamales!

Either stuffed inside a bread roll, fried or by itself, you can buy a tamal at pretty much every corner of the city. Before the workers leave their homes, the tamaleros are there – at bus stops, subway exits, crossroads, park entrances – waiting to feed them. Everyone has a tamalero of choice and stays loyal to them!

But hurry – they sell fast and the early morning rush hour is hungry! By 11 am it's hard to find the 'quick or takeaway' breakfast items, as the late breakfast culture has arrived with its bigger menu that's found in the fondas, cocinas economicas, restaurants, mercados, tianguis and eat-in kitchens throughout the city.

Breakfast items might also change according to the day of the week. It's common to have barbacoa (lamb), pancita (tripe soup) or quesadillas for breakfast on the weekend, but some of those stalls might not have a permanent spot in the street on a weekday. Instead they rotate, and can be found in different colonias (suburbs), alcaldias (regions) and country towns on different days.

HUEVOS RANCHEROS

RANCH EGGS

Huevos rancheros means 'ranch eggs' or 'countryside eggs' and you can usually ask for them even if they're not on the menu! Waitresses are always happy to pass on the request to the kitchen.

I make huevos rancheros at home when I have some leftover salsa – the recipe is for a mild salsa and perfect for anyone out there who prefers not to eat spicy food in the morning, and that includes me! But you can top the eggs with any taco salsa you like.

3 roma (plum) tomatoes, roughly chopped
½ white onion, roughly chopped
½ garlic clove
1 fresh jalapeno chilli, stalk removed, roughly chopped
1 teaspoon tomato paste (concentrated puree) (omit if you prefer a fresher salsa)
2 teaspoons table salt
8 Tortillas de maiz (see page 228)
vegetable oil spray
1 tablespoon vegetable oil
8 eggs
Frijoles negros or Frijoles refritos (see pages 226 or 227), to serve

Blitz the tomatoes, onion, garlic, jalapeno, tomato paste (if using), salt and 200 ml (7 fl oz) of water in a blender until you have a runny sauce. Transfer to a small saucepan and heat over low heat for about 5 minutes, until the sauce darkens and thickens slightly.

Heat a comal or frying pan over medium heat and spray the tortillas with vegetable oil spray. Working in batches, cook the tortillas for 1 minute each side or until heated through and starting to crisp (this prevents them going soggy when you add the sauce). Place two tortillas on each plate, slightly overlapping.

Heat the oil in a frying pan and fry the eggs until cooked to your liking. Serve one egg on top of each tortilla, top with the salsa and serve with frijoles negros or frijoles refritos on the side.

MOLLETES CON TOCINO

MOLLETES WITH BACON

Molletes are simple yet delicious. In my opinion, the pico de gallo topping is genius – it makes you lick your fingers and enjoy your molletes from first to last bite. I add a couple of extra chillies to my pico de gallo when it comes to molletes, because the mix of flavours can reduce the chilli heat.

This is the kind of breakfast I seek out whenever I visit Mexico – but I'm always happy to have it at home in Sydney, too!

If you prefer, you can replace the bacon with finely chopped ham or chorizo.

6 slices bacon, finely chopped
butter, for spreading
3 bolillos or crusty rolls, halved lengthways
½ x quantity Frijoles refritos (see page 227)
6 slices manchego, mozzarella or tasty cheese

To serve

1 x quantity Pico de gallo (see page 208)
coriander (cilantro) leaves
lime wedges

Heat a frying pan over medium heat, add the bacon, and cook, stirring occasionally, for about 5 minutes, until slightly crispy. Set aside.

Preheat a grill (broiler).

Lightly butter the bolillos or crusty rolls and place them under the grill, butter-side up, for about 2 minutes, until lightly toasted – you can also toast them in a frying pan over medium heat, butter-side down.

Thickly spread the frijoles refritos onto the rolls and top each half with a slice of cheese. Grill for 5–7 minutes, until the cheese is melted and golden.

Sprinkle the bacon over the cheese and top with the pico de gallo and a few coriander leaves. Serve with lime wedges on the side and get ready to start licking your fingers!

TAMALES FRITOS

FRIED TAMALES

MAKES 10

MAKES 10

Tamales are a culinary expression of dedication, patience, art and ancestral rituals all rolled into one! Steamed, they are completely delicious, but what happens when you take them to the next level and fry them too? I have only seen this done in Mexico City and only with corn-husked tamales – but why not? Let's dare!

500 g (1 lb 2 oz) boneless pork shoulder, cut into 5 cm (2 in) pieces
½ white onion
3 bay leaves
5 teaspoons table salt
10 large or 20 medium sweetcorn husks, plus extra if needed (see Note)
300 g (10½ oz) pork lard
1 teaspoon baking powder
500 g (1 lb 2 oz) masa flour
650 ml (22 fl oz) chicken stock, warmed
500 ml (2 cups) Salsa verde de chile asado (see page 209)

Place the pork, onion, bay leaves and 3 teaspoons of the salt in a saucepan and cover with water. Bring to the boil, then reduce the heat to low and simmer for about 1 hour, until the pork is tender. Allow the pork to cool in the stock, then transfer to a plate and shred the meat with two forks.

Soften the sweetcorn husks in warm water, then drain and squeeze the husks to remove any excess water.

Place 200 g (7 oz) of the lard and the baking powder in a large bowl and whip the mixture as fast as possible using a wooden spoon – the lard needs to soften and look spongy. Don't stress if this takes a long time; it can take up to 15 minutes to achieve the right consistency. Add the masa flour, warm chicken stock and remaining salt, and mix until you have a cohesive dough.

Spread 80 g (2¾ oz) of the dough in the middle of 1 large or 2 overlapping medium damp corn husks, leaving a 4 cm (1¼ in) border around the edge. Add 50 g (1¾ oz) of the shredded pork and 2½ tablespoons of the salsa verde, then cover with another 20 g (¾ oz) of dough. Wrap up the tamal by overlapping the sides of the husk and folding over the top and bottom edges towards the centre to enclose the filling (use an extra husk if needed). Secure the ends with kitchen string and set aside. Repeat with the remaining husks and ingredients.

Stand the tamales upright in a large steamer, but don't pack them in too tightly or they might burst. Place the steamer over a saucepan of simmering water and steam for 45 minutes or until the husks peel away easily. Allow the tamales to cool for 15 minutes, then unwrap them.

Melt the remaining lard in a frying pan over medium heat and, working in batches, fry the tamales for 3–4 minutes each side until golden and crispy.

NOTE

YOU CAN BUY DRIED SWEETCORN HUSKS FROM LATIN AMERICAN SUPERMARKETS OR ONLINE.

CHILAQUILES CON HUEVO

CHILAQUILES WITH EGGS

It's common in Mexico to find tortillas being dried in the sun, ready to be converted into delicious chilaquiles. There are infinite varieties: use your favourite salsa, soak your leftover totopos or tortillas, and add your favourite toppings.

In the city, chilaquiles are part of any kitchen's menu. Although the most common salsas are 'green', there's always an exciting chance of finding a rare salsa, like the ones made with pasilla or morita chillies. I recommend adding one of your favourite chillies to your preferred salsa for chilaquiles.

And, a word of advice: if you ever need a quick hangover cure, chilaquiles are definitely your solution!

2 x quantities Salsa verde de chile asado (see page 209)
½ x quantity Totopos (see page 232)
150 ml (5½ fl oz) thickened cream or sour cream
150 g (5½ oz) Cotija or feta, grated, plus extra to serve
½ white onion, diced
1 tablespoon vegetable oil
8 eggs
4 bolillos or crusty rolls
Frijoles refritos (see page 227), to serve
coriander (cilantro) leaves, to serve

Heat the salsa in a large frying pan over medium heat. Throw in the totopos, add 250 ml (1 cup) of water and cook, stirring frequently, for 5 minutes or until the totopos are fully soaked yet still crunchy in the middle. Remove the mixture from the heat (or keep stirring if you prefer soft chilaquiles), drizzle over the cream and top with the cheese and onion.

Meanwhile, heat the oil in a large frying pan over medium–high heat and fry the eggs to your liking.

Divide the chilaquiles among plates and top with the fried eggs. Serve with the bolillos or rolls and frijoles refritos on the side, along with a little extra grated cheese and a few coriander leaves scattered over the top.

CHILANGOLANDIA!
CHILANGOLANDIA!
CHILANGOLANDIA!
CHILANGOLANDIA!
CHILANGOLANDIA!
CHILANGOLANDIA!
CHILANGOLANDIA!

(IT REFERS TO MEXICO CITY)

IF YOU ARE FAMILIAR WITH THE MEXICAN LANGUAGE AND HAVE AT LEAST ONE FRIEND FROM MEXICO CITY, I'M SURE YOU HAVE HEARD THIS WORD BEFORE: CHILANGO(A), BUT WHAT IS THE MEANING OF IT?

Chilango is the nickname for someone living in CDMX. The history behind the name is unknown – although different Nahuatl or Mayan origins have been proffered over the years, they are still unconvincing. All I know is that people living in Mexico City are called 'chilangos' by Mexicans from other states; yet, 'citadinos' (people who were born and raised in the city) refers to all Mexican people from different states who have made their way to the city as chilangos! This is a funny confusion because we all came from somewhere to get to the city.

For example, if you asked me if I was a chilanga, I could probably say no, as I was born and raised in the city, making me a citadina. But my family background is from Puebla and Guerrero, so, if chilangos are outsiders in the city, what am I? I guess everyone in Mexico City has a background of traditions and culture from one of our beautiful states. In my very unique case, living in Australia, I feel proud of who I am, where I come from and the Mexican traditions I've brought to my now hometown, Sydney.

The Mexican capital has faced changes over the years. Until 2016, the city was well known by all as DF, meaning Distrito Federal. The name was used by millions of Mexicans for years, before it was changed to CDMX (Ciudad De México). Don't get confused – both names are correct and both refer to Mexico City, the crazy place full of colour, noise, art, music, food and hard-working people with caring hearts and big smiles, happy to make everyone feel welcome. Because mi casa es tu casa. And todos somos chilangos!

MIGAS CON HUEVO

CRUMBLED TORTILLA OMELETTE

Migas means 'crumbs', and this dish was given its name because the dried corn tortillas are cut into small crumbly pieces. When I lived with my mum in Mexico City she would cook this with my grandma in our kitchen.

I love its simplicity – the only ingredients you need here are tortillas, onion and eggs!

4 Tortillas de maiz (see page 228)
1½ tablespoons vegetable oil
1 white onion, finely chopped
6 eggs
1 teaspoon table salt
Frijoles refritos (see page 227), to serve
whole red chillies (optional), to serve

Leave the tortillas on a work surface in a single layer, uncovered, to dry out overnight. The next day, they should be a little dry around the edges, yet still be soft and edible. Alternatively, heat them up in a sandwich press for about 20 seconds – they will become slightly dehydrated and hard.

Cut the tortillas into 3 cm (1¼ in) squares.

Heat the oil in a frying pan over low heat, add the tortilla squares and stir for 2 minutes or until well coated in the oil. Add the onion and cook, stirring, for 5 minutes or until the onion is soft.

Beat the eggs with the salt and add to the onion and tortilla mixture. Cook, stirring the mixture gently, for 1–2 minutes, until the egg is set. Gently break up the egg, but do not overmix.

Divide the broken omelette among plates and serve with frijoles refritos on the side and a few whole red chillies, if you like.

HUEVOS A LA MEXICANA

SERVES 4

SERVES 4

MEXICAN EGGS

This healthy yet spicy breakfast is always on the menu, all over Mexico. Pretty much any dish with the word Mexicana or Mexicano in its name will be prepared with ingredients that contain the three colours of the national flag: green, white and red. In this case: green chilli, onion and tomato.

If you like mayonnaise, spread some over your tortilla before preparing your taco and thank me later!

1 tablespoon vegetable oil
½ white onion, diced
1 roma (plum) tomato, diced
2 green jalapeno or serrano chillies, diced
6 eggs, lightly beaten with a pinch of salt

To serve
sliced pickled jalapenos
Frijoles refritos (see page 227)
8 Tortillas de maiz (see page 228)
mayonnaise (optional)

Heat the oil in a frying pan over medium heat, add the onion, tomato and chilli and cook, stirring, for 2 minutes or until the onion and chilli are soft. Add the egg and stir gently for about 3 minutes until the egg sets and scrambles.

Divide the scrambled eggs among plates and scatter with a few slices of pickled jalapeno. Serve with frijoles refritos and tortillas on the side, spreading the tortillas with mayonnaise, if you like.

QUESADILLAS CON HONGOS

MUSHROOM QUESADILLAS

What kind of Mexican would I be if I didn't include a recipe for breakfast quesadillas?

Quesadillas ... from Monday to Sunday, all day long and with a huge variety of fillings. You can find them everywhere – outside metro stations, at corner stalls, next to tamales stands, at street markets, the garage of your neighbour, around the church ... It doesn't matter what time of day it is, quesadillas are always a good option!

With or without cheese? That's the question when ordering a quesadilla in Mexico City – it's the big difference between quesadillas from the city and the states. Yes, we have quesadillas without cheese ... and they are delicious! Blue, white or yellow corn for your tortilla dough? It's your choice! I like to use blue in this recipe.

1 tablespoon vegetable oil
¼ white onion, diced
250 g (9 oz) button mushrooms, finely sliced
1 green jalapeno or serrano chilli, finely chopped
pinch of table salt
vegetable oil spray
8 Tortilla de maiz, made with blue masa flour
  (see page 228)
240 g (8½ oz) Oaxaca cheese or firm
  mozzarella, grated or shredded
Salsa verde de chile asado (see page 209),
  to serve

Heat the oil in a frying pan over medium heat, add the onion and saute for about 3 minutes, until soft. Add the mushroom, chilli and salt and saute for 5 minutes or until soft.

Lightly spray a comal or heavy-based frying pan with oil spray and place over medium heat.

Working in batches, add the tortillas and cook for about 3 minutes, until the edge of each tortilla is lightly golden. Flip, add 30 g (1 oz) of the cheese and one-eighth of the mushroom mixture to one side of each tortilla, then fold in half and cook for 2 minutes. Flip again and continue to cook until the cheese is melted.

Serve the quesadillas with salsa verde on the side for an added kick.

HUEVOS AL ALBANIL

BRICKLAYERS' EGGS

SERVES 4

SERVES 4

Bricklayers' eggs! The preferred breakfast of tradies ... super-spicy and juicy and just what's needed before a long day of hard work in the chaotic city. This is what we call the dish in Mexico City, anyway – in other parts of the country it's known simply as 'huevos con salsa'. It's a dish that can be made a thousand different ways and probably deserves its own chapter in this book!

And it's not just for tradies – served with warm homemade tortillas and perhaps slices of panela cheese, this is a common breakfast throughout CDMX.

1 tablespoon vegetable oil
4 roma (plum) tomatoes, cut into quarters
½ white onion
2 green jalapeno or serrano chillies
1 garlic clove
table salt
vegetable oil spray
6 eggs, lightly beaten
2 fresh chiles de árbol (see Note)

To serve

Frijoles refritos (see page 227)
Tortillas de maiz (see page 228)
Salsa verde de chile asado (see page 209)
lime wedges

Heat the oil in a comal or heavy-based frying pan over medium heat, add the tomato, onion, chillies and garlic and cook, stirring occasionally, for about 7 minutes, until slightly charred. Transfer the charred vegetables to a blender, add 1 teaspoon of salt and 450 ml (15 fl oz) of water and blend until smooth – the sauce will be quite runny.

Spray a large frying pan with vegetable oil spray and place over medium–low heat. Add the egg and cook, stirring gently, for 4 minutes or until lightly scrambled. Stir through the tomato and chilli sauce and throw in the whole chiles de árbol. Cover with a lid, reduce the heat to low and cook for 5 minutes.

Divide the scrambled egg among bowls and serve with frijoles refritos, tortillas, salsa verde and lime wedges. (You can eat the chiles de árbol!)

NOTE

FRESH CHILES DE ÁRBOL CAN BE PURCHASED FROM SPECIALTY MEXICAN GROCERS; FRESH JALAPENO CHILLIES ARE A GOOD SUBSTITUTE.

SINCRONIZADAS

FLOUR TORTILLA SANDWICHES

Despite opinions about flour tortillas 'not being Mexican' or not being eaten in all parts of the country, this is a common breakfast dish. It combines flour tortillas from the north with city style to make something quick and delicious.

I ate sincronizadas almost every morning at my high-school canteen. They were topped with a super-spicy, lemony guacamole, and enjoyed with coffee – and, of course, my friend Araceli by my side!

800 g (1 lb 12 oz) Oaxaca cheese
   or firm mozzarella, grated
1 x quantity Tortillas de harina (see page 229)
10 slices ham
Guacamole, to serve (see page 213)

Divide the cheese among half the tortillas, top with a slice of ham and then the remaining tortillas (as if you're making a round sandwich).

Heat a comal or heavy-based frying pan over low heat. Working in batches, cook the sincronizadas, flipping regularly, for about 2 minutes, until the cheese is melted. Don't let the sincronizadas burn.

Top the sincronizadas with guacamole and serve!

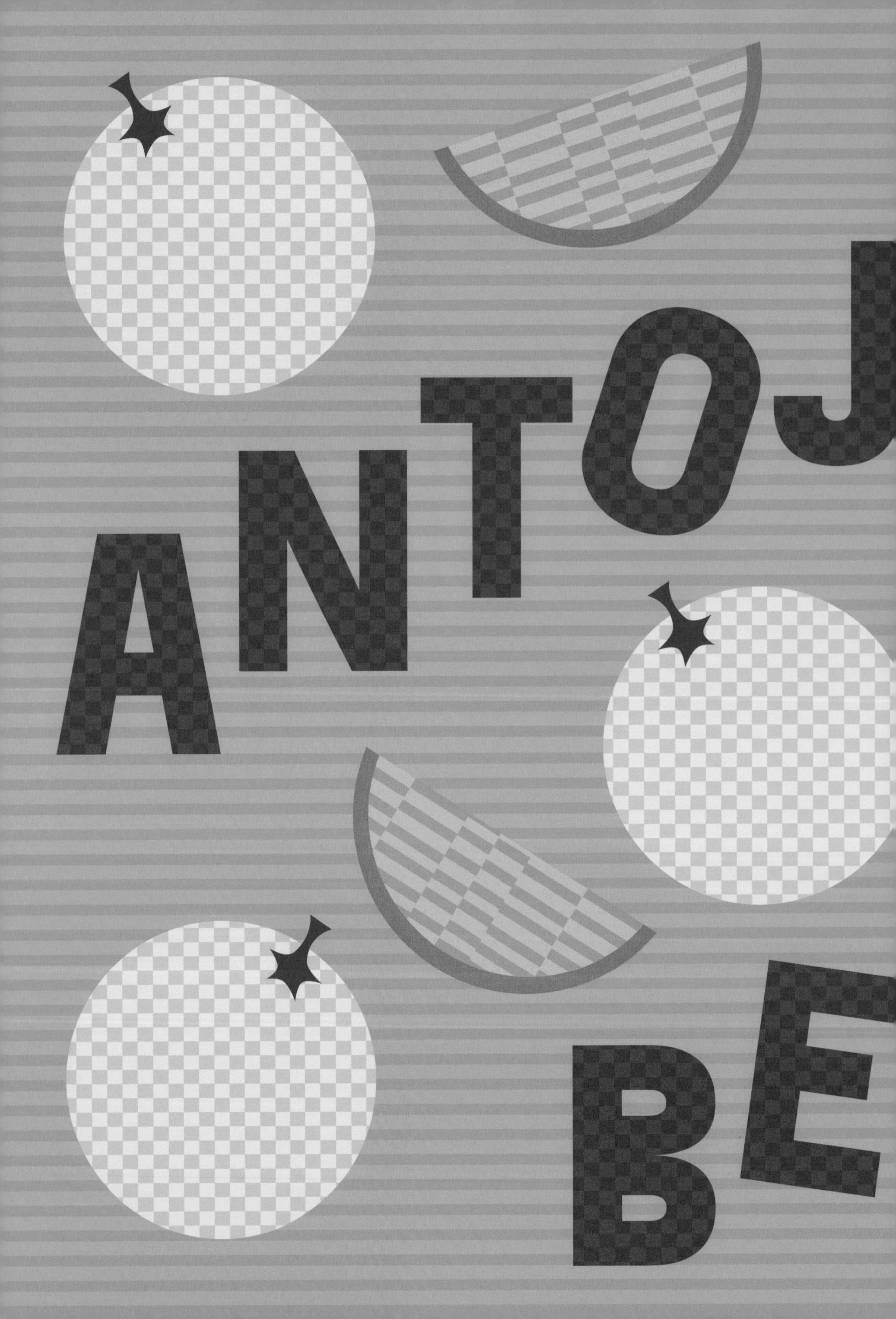
ANTOJ
BE

ITOS
Y
BIDAS
DAS

ANTOJITOS Y BEBIDAS

EAT,

'A beber y

DRINK AND

a tragar que el

BE MERRY, FOR

mundo se va a acabar.'

TOMORROW WE DIE!

What I love most about visiting Mexico and walking around the streets is discovering all the new snacks, drinks and crazy exotic mixtures, creations or ingredients that have become a trend. After a few years in the mercados, they become part of the Mexican pantry, and some of them even make their way to the very top – being served and improved upon at fancy gourmet restaurants.

Snacks and drinks are different all over the country, but the city – the place where most immigrants and country-town people end up living – makes all the variations even bigger and funkier. Ingredients and ideas converge there from everywhere. Sometimes they are as simple as fruit with chamoy or as crazy as a new Cheeto powder topping for colourful chilli lollies, or fluorescent blue alcoholic drinks with chilli gummies and blueberry powder.

Not everything is alcohol and chilli; we also have a range of fruit drinks – aguas frescas. There will usually be up to 20 options, with the most popular being Jamaica (hibiscus iced tea) and horchata. These beauties can be found at every ice creamery, street market stall, school canteen and from the walking sellers at traffic lights.

The diversity of snacks and drinks also have their own timeframe – some are only available in the morning, while others are night owls. It doesn't matter what time of the day you wander around, don't be afraid to try them, even if they look radioactive!

If you're after traditional snacks (botanas) and drinks (which are, by the way, a very good and easy option), I highly recommend visiting old cantinas. These bars are found throughout the city – some might look dodgy from the outside but I guarantee that almost all of them are divine on the inside, with classy decoration from French touches to American styles. Cantinas have been trading for years: they are favourite Mexican spaces where leisure and pleasure are combined with music, food and a large variety of drinks. None is the same as any other, and they all have their own personality, character and even signature dishes. They can make chilangos travel from top to bottom of the metro line to eat the delicacies that are only served in their one favourite cantina.

Botanas are usually served for free when you are drinking in a cantina. Sometimes this might be just peanuts with chilli powder, or wheat chicharrones with Valentina sauce, but the more drinks you order, the better botanas they bring!

ESQUITES CON TUETANO

CORN IN A CUP WITH MARROWBONES

Esquites are one of the chilango's favourite mid-evening snacks. On any day of the week you will find the elotero outside churches, bakeries, supermarkets – or perhaps just at the corner of your street – with his humble yet powerful corn trolley packed with massive mayo jars, chilli powders, cheese, limes, salt and take-away containers. The steam rising from the boiling pot spreads over the city streets, inviting Mexicans to buy a little piece of heaven, relax and forget about any daily stresses.

I put the traditional recipe for esquites in my first cookbook *Comida Mexicana*, as I think it's important to understand the basics. But, bit by bit, you can add more ingredients, so here I'm adding marrowbones, to take this snack to the next level.

My friend Luis invited me to a place near his house where they serve esquites with a very spicy sauce. The hot corn and spiciness together scorched my soul – I enjoyed it so much! Try adding salsa de siete chiles to this one and see what happens!

2 teaspoons unsalted butter
2 teaspoons table salt
2 teaspoons dried epazote leaves (optional)
3 white or yellow sweetcorn cobs, husks and silks removed, kernels stripped (about 450 g/1 lb kernels)
4 x 5 cm (2 in) pieces beef marrowbones
80 g (⅓ cup) whole egg mayonnaise
juice of 4 limes, plus lime wedges to serve
100 g (3½ oz) queso fresco, Cotija or feta, crumbled
cayenne pepper or Tajin seasoning, for sprinkling
Salsa de siete chiles (see page 217), to serve

Melt the butter in a large saucepan over medium heat and add the salt and epazote (if using). Add the corn kernels and cook, stirring frequently, for 10 minutes or until lightly golden. Add 2 litres (2 qts) of water and the marrowbones, then cover and cook, stirring occasionally and making sure the ingredients remain completely submerged, for 1 hour or until the marrow is popping out of the bones (add more water if necessary).

To serve, divide half the corn kernels among four cups, leaving most of the stock behind. Stir half the mayonnaise, half the lime juice and half the cheese through the corn kernels and sprinkle with cayenne pepper or Tajin. Add 1½ tablespoons of stock to each cup, then top with the remaining corn kernels, mayo, lime juice and cheese, and a good amount of salsa de siete chiles. Finish with a marrowbone and serve with lime wedges on the side.

ELOTES CON CHEETOS

CHEETOS-DUSTED SWEETCORN

Street vendors in Mexico city strive to keep their snacks and street food innovative, attractive and fun in order to attract customers and keep up to date with new ingredients familiar to those moving from the countryside to the city to find a better life.

The last time I was in CDMX in early 2022, I found these colourful elotes at one of my favourite stalls. Trying them was a funky experience and a explosion of flavours that you should try at least once!

300 g (10½ oz) cheese corn puffs
   or cheese-flavoured corn chips
6 white or yellow sweetcorn cobs,
   husks and silks removed
3 teaspoons table salt
250 g (1 cup) whole egg mayonnaise

Crush the corn puffs or corn chips to a powder either using a blender or a mortar and pestle. Tip onto a large plate and spread out.

Bring a large saucepan of water to the boil over high heat. Add the corn and salt, then reduce the heat to a simmer and cook for 10 minutes or until the corn is tender and cooked through. Drain the corn and allow it to steam in the pan for 5 minutes, until completely dry (you can also dry the corn with a clean tea towel, if you prefer). Skewer each end of the corn with metal forks or thick wooden skewers.

Brush the corn with the mayonnaise, then roll in the crushed corn puffs or corn chips to coat.

ESQUITES
CON TUETANO
PAGE 42

ELOTES CON CHEETOS

PAGE 43

ALITAS DE POLLO

CHICKEN WINGS

I have a secret! I used to be a fussy eater when I lived in Mexico. I didn't even eat chicken wings until I was a teenager. Nowadays it's the complete opposite – I feel like I missed so many years of trying new things and want to make up for it. I love alitas and all the toppings that come with them. We have such a variety of sauces – just imagine how many different types of alitas we could create! Chillies, dips and salsas are just a few of the toppings you could use. Here I've used habanero and mango salsa to match with the chicken wings.

20 chicken wings, drumettes and
  wingettes separated
35 g (¼ cup) plain (all-purpose) flour
1 teaspoon sweet paprika
2 teaspoons table salt
500 ml (2 cups) vegetable oil
1 x quantity Salsa de habanero con mango
  (see page 221)
2 teaspoons brown sugar
1½ tablespoons white vinegar
2 teaspoons olive oil

Clean the chicken wings, then place them in a bowl and add the flour, paprika and half the salt. Cover the bowl with plastic wrap, then shake the bowl to fully coat the chicken in the flour mixture.

Heat the vegetable oil in a very large heavy-based saucepan over high heat to 200°C (400°F) on a kitchen thermometer. Add half the wings to the hot oil and cook, turning occasionally, for 15 minutes or until they are dark golden and very crisp. Using a slotted spoon, remove the wings and transfer to a tray lined with paper towel to drain. Bring the oil back to temperature and cook the remaining chicken wings.

Meanwhile, whisk the salsa, sugar, remaining salt, the vinegar and 1½ tablespoons of water in a bowl until combined. Heat the olive oil in a saucepan over medium heat, add the sauce and cook, stirring, for 2–3 minutes, until heated through.

Place the wings in a large serving bowl, add most of the sauce and toss to combine. Serve immediately, with the remaining sauce drizzled over the top.

PICADITAS DE FRIJOL

BEAN PICADITAS

This dish will always remind me of holidays in Veracruz, where picaditas can be found in any mercado or kitchen. They are similar to sopes – the only difference is the toppings. The thickness is the same, and the size depends on you. I prefer to make my picaditas smaller than sopes, as they are meant to be light and easy to eat. You will find them offered as botanas (snacks) at some city bars.

1 kg (2 lb 3 oz) Tortilla dough (see page 228)
1 tablespoon Frijoles refritos (see page 227)
oil cooking spray
200 g (7 oz) Salsa verde de chile asado (see page 209)
1 white onion, finely diced

Place the tortilla dough in a large bowl, add the frijoles refritos and mix with your hands until well combined.

Lightly spray a comal or heavy-based frying pan with oil spray and place over medium–high heat.

Place a square of plastic wrap over the bottom half of a tortilla press. Roll 100 g (3½ oz) of the dough into a ball and place it in the middle of the press. Cover with another square of plastic wrap, then close the press and gently press to flatten the dough into a 1 cm (⅓ in) thick picadita.

Open the tortilla press, remove the top layer of plastic wrap and flip the picadita onto your hand. Remove the bottom layer of plastic wrap and place the picadita in the comal or pan. Cook for about 3 minutes each side until firm.

Fill a small bowl with cold water. Remove the picadita from the pan and place it on a clean work surface. Dip your fingers in the water, then pinch the edge of the picadita to form a rim. Repeat with the remaining dough to make about 10 picaditas.

Top the picaditas with the salsa and onion, and enjoy!

JALAPENOS RELLENOS DE QUESO

CHEESE-STUFFED JALAPENOS

The last time I was in Mexico City, my friend Juan Ma took me to a hotdog stall and these stuffed chillies were my favourite snack. The smell was luring us in from several blocks away and the smoke coming from the grill was tantalising as we waited for our order to appear. It is an experience I'd recommend! You can find hotdog stalls in the evenings in Mexico City's bar and nightclub areas – the stalls move around so it's hard to pinpoint an exact spot. Roma, Condesa, Zona Rosa and Centro are always good areas to party – so keep your eyes open there!

10 green jalapeno chillies, stalks intact
200 g (7 oz) cream cheese, softened
1 teaspoon table salt
1 teaspoon ground white pepper
10 slices streaky bacon

Cut a long lengthways slit down one side of each jalapeno chilli and use a teaspoon to scrape out the seeds and membrane.

Bring a saucepan of salted water to the boil, add the chillies and cook for 10 minutes or until soft. Drain and set aside to cool.

Mix the cream cheese, salt and white pepper in a bowl until the cheese is creamy and spreadable. Using a teaspoon, stuff the cream cheese mixture into the cooled jalapeno chillies. Close up the slits and wrap each jalapeno with a slice of streaky bacon. Secure with toothpicks.

Heat a comal or heavy-based frying pan over medium heat and cook the stuffed jalapenos, turning frequently, for about 7 minutes, until the bacon is crispy. Serve hot.

TOSTADAS DE FRIJOL

BEAN TOSTADAS

Tostadas de frijol are always a good option for a light and nutritious meal that's easy to make. It is common to find them at weekday markets, where vendors give them away so you can try their products before buying, but the ones we are making here are a bit more elaborate, with extra toppings and crunchy ingredients to add a fresh bite.

I remember eating tostadas de frijol in my mum's home town Agua Fria, where my aunt Luz would make a bunch of them to feed us using her basic Mexican pantry ingredients, including a delicious ranch cheese that she used to make from scratch every day. The tostadas were made with leftover tortillas that were sometimes dried in the sun and sometimes deep-fried. Both are memorable and humble and definitely a must for this cookbook.

1 x quantity Frijoles refritos (see page 227)
10 Tostadas (see page 233)
1 iceberg lettuce, finely shredded
250 ml (1 cup) thickened cream
200 g (7 oz) queso fresco, panela, Cotija or feta, crumbled
Salsa verde de chile asado (see page 209), to serve

Spread a thick layer of frijoles refritos over each tostada and top with a handful of shredded lettuce, a drizzle of cream and the crumbled cheese. Finish with the salsa verde and serve.

TOSTADAS DE QUESO

CHEESE TOSTADAS

I usually make these tostadas to enjoy as a snack whenever I have tortillas leftover at home, and they are always a success. The first time I had something similar was at a kids' party in Mexico City. I haven't seen or found anything like them at street food stalls, but I wanted to include them in this book as they are delightful and a wonderful vegetarian option.

cooking oil spray
400 g (14 oz) haloumi, cut into thick rectangular slices
4 avocados
1 tablespoon olive oil
1 teaspoon table salt
10 Tostadas (see page 233)
½ x quantity Pico de gallo (see page 208)
1 x quantity Jalapenos toreados (see page 238)

Heat a comal or heavy-based frying pan over medium heat and spray with oil. Add the haloumi and cook for about 2 minutes each side, until lightly golden. Remove from the pan.

Mash the avocados and stir through the olive oil and salt. Spread a thick layer of the mashed avocado onto each tostada and top with two slices of haloumi. Spoon the pico de gallo over the haloumi and serve with the jalapenos toreados on the side.

TOSTADAS DE COCHINITA PIBIL

PULLED-PORK TOSTADAS

Cochinita pibil (pulled pork) is originally from Yucatan and it's the most popular Mayan dish in Mexico. In Mexico City, El Turix is my favourite place to go for this dish – it has the best texture, consistency, flavour and, of course, colour from the onion and habanero salsa. The small street food stall sits outside a famous cemetery where my ancestors are buried, along with famous singers, painters and artists, including the much-loved actor and singer María Félix.

Going to my family's graveyard is always an emotional experience, especially because I don't live in Mexico City anymore. A tostada de cochinita pibil at the end of the visit is always comforting and makes me feels like I have my family all around me, enjoying a bite or two.

150 g (5½ oz) achiote paste
2½ tablespoons white vinegar
2½ tablespoons bitter or regular orange juice
1 tablespoon table salt
1 kg (2 lb 3 oz) boneless pork shoulder or leg, cut into 5 cm (2 in) chunks
1 banana leaf
10 Tostadas (see page 233)
1 x quantity Frijoles refritos (see page 227)
Salsa de habanero con mango (see page 221) or Salsa de zanahoria con habanero (see page 220), to serve

Pickled red onion

2 red onions, finely sliced
1 tablespoon dried Mexican oregano
1 teaspoon table salt
2 tablespoons white vinegar
1 teaspoon freshly squeezed lemon juice

Place the achiote paste, vinegar, orange juice and salt in the small bowl of a food processor or blender and blend to a thick paste.

Place the pork in a large bowl and rub the achiote paste into the meat. Cover and set aside in the fridge to marinate for at least 3 hours.

Preheat the oven to 220°C (430°F).

Place the marinated pork in a roasting tin in a single layer, cover with the banana leaf (this adds flavour to the meat) and then foil, and roast for 1 hour or until tender.

Meanwhile, to make the pickled red onion, bring a saucepan of water to the boil. Add the onion and blanch for 1 minute, then drain and immediately plunge into iced water to stop the cooking process. Drain again and place in a bowl with the oregano, salt, vinegar and lemon juice. Stir to combine.

Remove the pork from the oven and discard the foil and banana leaf. Reduce the temperature to 150°C (300°F), return the pork to the oven and cook for a further 15 minutes or until browned. Using two forks, gently pull or shred the pork.

Spread a thick layer of frijoles refritos over each tostada and top with the pulled pork. Finish with the pickled onion and your choice of salsa, to taste, and serve with lime wedges on the side.

TOSTADAS DE PICADILLO DE SOYA

SOY TOSTADAS

Tostadas de picadillo are commonly enjoyed on Día de la Independencia de México (Mexico Independence Day), when we celebrate with food, music, family, friends and tequila.

I often use TVP (Textured Vegetable Protein) for my vegan or vegetarian diners and I've found it is the perfect replacement for chorizo, meatballs and, in this case, picadillo. I love to make these with a nice spread of sour cream, but you can also swap the cream for refried beans.

500 g (1 lb 2 oz) TVP (Textured Vegetable Protein)
5 roma (plum) tomatoes, roughly chopped
2 carrots, cut into 1 cm (⅓ in) dice
2 potatoes, cut into 1 cm (⅓ in) dice
2 tablespoons vegetable oil
2 garlic cloves
1 brown onion, finely diced, plus ½ onion extra
1 teaspoon table salt
1 teaspoon freshly ground black pepper
250 ml (1 cup) vegetable stock
2 bay leaves
1 sweetcorn cob, husks and silks removed, kernels stripped
100 g (3½ oz) green beans, trimmed

To serve

250 g (1 cup) sour cream
10 Tostadas (see page 233)
1 iceberg lettuce, shredded
2 avocados, finely sliced
200 g (7 oz) queso fresco, panela, Cotija or feta, crumbled
Salsa de siete chiles (see page 217)
lime wedges

Place the TVP in a bowl and cover with warm water. Set aside for 15 minutes to hydrate, then drain.

Place the tomato and 500 ml (2 cups) of water in a saucepan and bring to the boil over medium heat. Cook for 10 minutes or until soft, then remove using a slotted spoon and set aside to cool. Add the carrot and potato to the water and cook for 7 minutes, until par-cooked, then strain the liquid, reserving 250 ml (1 cup). Allow the carrot and potato to cool.

Heat the oil in a frying pan over medium heat, add one garlic clove and cook until slightly burnt (this adds a bitter edge to the sauce), then remove and discard. Add the finely diced onion to the pan and saute for 5 minutes, then add the hydrated TVP and salt and stir to combine. Reduce the heat to low and cook for 10 minutes to warm through.

Place the tomato, the remaining garlic clove, onion half, black pepper and vegetable stock in a blender and blend until smooth. Pour the mixture over the TVP and add the bay leaves, corn, beans, carrot and potato. Cook, stirring occasionally, for 10 minutes or until the vegetables are cooked through.

Spread a thick layer of sour cream over each tostada and top with a good amount of the TVP picadillo. Finish with the iceberg lettuce, avocado, cheese and a good amount of salsa, and serve with lime wedges on the side.

GORDITAS DE QUESO ENCHILADO

CHILLI CHEESE CORN POCKETS

Gorditas, meaning 'little chubby', is the cute name given to this dish and accurately describes these thick tortillas stuffed with different ingredients. The most traditional gorditas in Mexico City are made with chicharrón prensado or what I call 'soft pork crackling', but nowadays you will find them filled with carnitas, suadero, queso, pastor and much more. There are many ways to make gorditas, from grilled to deep-fried, with blue, yellow, white and even green dough, depending on their preparation.

500 g (1 lb 2 oz) masa flour
pinch of table salt
1 tablespoon guajillo chilli powder
    or sweet paprika
2½ tablespoons vegetable oil
cooking oil spray
Guacamole (see page 213), to serve
lime wedges, to serve

Gordita filling

4 dried guajillo chillies
2 dried chile de árbol
½ white onion, roughly chopped
150 g (5½ oz) fresh ricotta
100 g (3½ oz) haloumi, finely diced
200 g (7 oz) pickled jalapenos, finely diced

To make the gordita filling, place the dried chillies in a saucepan with 750 ml (3 cups) of water and bring to the boil over high heat. Boil the chillies for 5–7 minutes, until soft, then remove using a slotted spoon and reserve the cooking water. Set the chillies aside to cool.

Blend the chillies, onion and 100 ml (3½ fl oz) of the chilli cooking water in a blender until smooth. Transfer to a bowl and add the ricotta, haloumi and pickled jalapenos, and mix until well combined.

To make the dough, place the masa flour, salt, chilli powder or sweet paprika and vegetable oil in a large bowl. Add 600 ml (20½ fl oz) of the chilli cooking water and mix with your hands until you have a soft and non-sticky dough.

Roll 100 g (3½ oz) of the dough into a ball, then gently flatten with your hand. Place 30 g (1 oz) of the chilli cheese mixture in the centre. Fold the dough over the filling and roll into a large ball. Flatten the ball on a work surface using both hands until is about 10–12 cm (4–4¾ in) in diameter. Repeat to make 12 gorditas.

Heat a comal or heavy-based frying pan over medium–high heat and spray with oil. Working in batches, cook the gorditas, flipping frequently, for 8–10 minutes, until lightly golden. Top with guacamole and serve with lime wedges.

GORDITAS DE FRIJOL

BLACK BEAN GORDITAS

This recipe is dedicated to the memory of my beloved abuelita, Angelita, who taught me how to make this simple and humble dish. The ingredients are not in any way fancy, but the flavour is definitely full of love.

My friends from Los Troncos were always excited when my abuelita came to visit from her hometown, as she enjoyed bringing her local ingredients to feed us, as well as sharing her culinary skills.

360 g (12½ oz) Frijoles negros (see page 226)
1 x quantity Tortilla dough (see page 228)
cooking oil spray
Salsa de cacahuate y chile de arbol
  (see page 216), to serve
thickened cream or sour cream, to serve

Drain the beans, reserving 100 ml (3½ fl oz) of the cooking water, then place the beans in a large bowl with the tortilla dough. Mash the dough and beans together, adding a little of the bean stock if the mixture is very dry, and mix with your hands to form a soft and non-sticky dough.

Roll 100 g (3½ oz) of the dough into a ball and gently flatten it into a disc no bigger than the size of your hand. Repeat with the remaining dough to make 12 gorditas.

Heat a comal or heavy-based frying pan over medium–high heat and spray with oil. Working in batches, cook the gorditas, flipping frequently, for 8–10 minutes, until lightly golden.

Top the gorditas with salsa, to taste, and a drizzle of cream. Serve warm.

DORILOCOS

This snack mix is an everyday treat for many Mexicans. It's sold throughout the streets from stalls outside nightclubs, schools and offices, at street fairs and even at some corner shops. And you can add more ingredients to satisfy your own personal cravings!

I remember eating potato chips with a lot of added Valentina and Botanera sauce, lime juice and salt when I was in primary school. Don Papas was a cool guy who rode a bike laden with perfectly organised snacks in small plastic bags. The trick was to add all the sauces and squeeze them down enough so that you could tie a knot in the top of the bag. You'd then tear open the bottom of the bag with your teeth and suck out the soupy chips, which by this time would be soft and deliciously soaked in chilli sauce!

170 g (6 oz) bag Doritos Cheese Supreme
   or cheese-flavoured corn chips
150 g (5½ oz) bag Mafer lemon-roasted peanuts
   or Japanese-style Mexican peanuts (optional)
70 g (½ cup) salted peanuts
45 g (1¼ oz) Cheetos or cheese puffs
1 tablespoon Valentina hot sauce
1 teaspoon Maggi seasoning
juice of 1 large lime
1 carrot, shredded
1 long cucumber, cut into 1 cm (⅓ in) dice
2 teaspoons Chamoy salsa (see page 222;
   or use store-bought)
1 teaspoon Tajin seasoning

All you need to do is cut open the Doritos bag lengthways using a pair of scissors, then add the remaining ingredients.

Hold the open sides of the bag together and give everything a shake, then put the bag in the middle of the table for everyone to enjoy!

TIP

FEEL FREE TO ADD MORE
OF YOUR FAVOURITE SAUCES!

MICHELADA CUBANA

CUBAN MICHELADA

Like a cold beer? Would you dare to add a few interesting tangy ingredients to it? Micheladas have been on Mexican drinks menus for years and we're always coming up with new ingredients to add.

When we talk about micheladas in my family, we all have different opinions. Mum and Dad don't like anything extra in their beer other than just lime and salt, while my sister drinks her micheladas with a bunch of seafood in the glass ... more like a seafood cocktail, and, yes, it is delicious!

I was surprised on my last visit to the city when I saw blue, pink and green micheladas decorated with funny gummies and tamarind lollies. The flavours and colours are endless, and it is a drink you must try at least once if you are in CDMX.

With the recipe below, always remember you can also add toppings to your glass or bottle rim, such as caramelised sesame seeds or crushed peanuts, chilli gummies, pulparindo (tamarind candy), chilli lollipops, fruit slices and even prawns (shrimp), like my sister does!

2 teaspoons Chamoy salsa (see page 222; or use store-bought)
3 shakes of Tajin seasoning, plus extra for sprinkling
1 teaspoon Miguelito powder, original flavour
2 pinches of table salt
juice of 2 limes
80 ml (⅓ cup) clamato juice
1 teaspoon Tabasco sauce
1 teaspoon Maggi seasoning
1 teaspoon Worcestershire sauce
355 ml (12 fl oz) bottle Mexican lager

Combine the chamoy, Tajin seasoning, Miguelito powder and a pinch of salt in a small bowl. Dip the rim of a tall beer glass into the mixture, then sprinkle with more Tajin.

Add the lime juice, the remaining pinch of salt, clamato juice, Tabasco, Maggi seasoning and Worcestershire sauce to the glass and stir, making sure that the salt is fully dissolved. Add the beer and enjoy!

DORILOCOS
PAGE 70

MICHELADA
CUBANA
PAGE 71

PEPINOS RELLENOS

CUCUMBER SHOTS

The original of this dish is on the drinks menu at La Ópera Cantina, which opened more than 100 years ago and has hosted politicians, revolutionary warriors, artists, singers and more. This great fresh snack, amazingly, has its origins with Pancho Villa, our (either much-hated or much-loved) general in the Mexican Revolution. He was well known as the first Mexican to lead an invasion in the USA.

Urban legend tells how Pancho Villa, Porfirio Diaz and Emiliano Zapata would meet, drink and eat at La Ópera, planning a revolution in the middle of a bar that even nowadays maintains its ornate hand-shaped mahogany furniture and gold leaf – and, of course, the famous bullet hole in the ceiling made by this iconic revolutionary, 'El Centauro del Norte'.

2 large long thick cucumbers
2 teaspoons Chamoy salsa (see page 222;
   or use store-bought)
2 teaspoons Tajin seasoning or chilli powder
juice of 2 limes
table salt
4 x 30 ml (1 fl oz) shots white tequila

Cut the cucumbers in half widthways so you have four pieces, then slice off the rounded ends – we are going to use the cucumbers as shot glasses!

Using a long-handled teaspoon, carefully scoop out and dispose of the seeds and watery parts of the cucumber, being careful not to go all the way through. Dip the rim of the cucumbers in the chamoy and then the Tajin. Divide the lime juice among the cucumber 'shot glasses' and add a pinch of salt. Top with a shot of tequila and serve.

Once you've finished the tequila, you eat the cucumber 'glass'!

PALOMA

Despite margaritas being the most popular tequila cocktail around the world, I'd say that palomas and muppets are more commonly drunk by Mexicans. The increasing number of tourists visiting CDMX pushes bar owners to include margaritas on their menus, either frozen or on the rocks. However, I invite you to try a paloma for your next tequila night!

It can be tricky to make palomas outside Mexico, as the main ingredient is a soft drink with a unique grapefruit flavour that is refreshingly crisp and sweet – perfect for this cocktail. Its name is Squirt and, even though it was created in the USA, it's made in Mexico with sugar cane. In Sydney I use a commercial grapefruit soda and add fresh lime juice. So don't be worried if you're missing Squirt – there is always a solution for it!

table salt, for the rim
juice of 2 limes, plus 1 lime wedge
handful of ice cubes
30 ml (1 fl oz) white tequila
200 ml (7 fl oz) grapefruit soda

Place some salt on a plate. Rub the lime wedge around the rim of a glass, then press the rim into the salt. Fill the glass with ice cubes, then add the tequila, grapefruit soda and lime juice and stir to combine. Enjoy straight away.

HORCHATA

I love the description of horchata by one of my staff members, who refers to it as 'Mexican rice pudding shake'! This sweet creamy iced drink is a Mexican favourite, although its origins lie in Spain, where it was made with a different ingredient called 'chufa'. The most popular version in Mexico City is made with rice, and in other states it's made with almonds, soybeans, coconut or sesame seeds. There is a very specific market stall at the Mercado de Azcapotzalco where they add extra cinnamon to the mix, and sprinkle more on top to serve – I had very strong cravings for it when I was pregnant!

50 g (¼ cup) jasmine rice
1.5 litres (51 fl oz) just boiled water
3 tablespoons condensed milk
3 tablespoons evaporated milk
1 teaspoon ground cinnamon
ice cubes, to serve

Place the rice in a heatproof bowl or jar and add the boiled water. Stir and set aside to cool to room temperature. The rice will soften slightly.

Transfer the rice and soaking water to a blender and blend until the rice is finely chopped and almost dissolved.

Strain the liquid into a large bowl or jar and discard any remaining bits of rice. Add the milks and cinnamon, stir well and refrigerate for 30 minutes.

Add 500 ml (2 cups) of water to the horchata and stir it all together. Serve, poured over ice.

78   ANTOJITOS Y BEBIDAS

TACOS TACOS

one
Eat tacos with your hands, never use cutlery!

two
Add salsa and lime juice - always.

three
Hold your taco from side to side using three fingers (thumb, index and middle).

four
Elbows up! Make a triangle between your chest and mouth.

TACO

How to hold and eat a taco

RULES

five
Tilt your head at a 45-degree angle to your shoulder.

six
Take a good bite. Repeat!

seven
Hold your plate up to your chest to catch any filling that falls out of the taco.

eight
And always remember: 'En la forma de agarrar el taco se identifica al tragon!'*

*'By the way he attacks his taco, the glutton reveals himself!'

The best definition for tacos is to call them a gift from the gods! They are a Mexican addiction that does not respect gender, age, geography or financial status. We *all* love tacos!

The legend of Quetzalcoatl tells the story of bringing corn, the unreachable golden seed, from the top of the mountain to the Aztecs so they could use it as food and avoid hunger forever. So, tortillas made with corn are definitely the best gift from Quetzalcoatl to the world.

Of course, nixtamalisation is an important process – without it, tortillas wouldn't exist and, without them, tacos wouldn't exist. There are no documents or written stories about the creation or invention of nixtamal. Seriously, who had the marvellous idea of soaking corn with slaked lime, cooking it to make masa, rolling the masa into little balls and then flattening and cooking the balls on hot rocks to make tortillas? All we know for certain is that tortillas are now the mainstay of every Mexican meal from the top to the bottom of the country, with every kind of filling. Tortillas are versatile and can be made with blue, yellow, white or any colour corn.

Historically, tacos were created when the Aztecs used tortillas as cutlery to grab beans with, then topped them with small fish and chilli. When the Spanish arrived, they added different ingredients, such as pork, which was introduced to Mesoamerica after the conquest by Cortés. We could probably say that carnitas were the first meat tacos in existence and they are still on our street-food menus today.

The structure of the taco is simple – it consists of tortilla, filling and toppings. Simple, yet delicious, and with an almost unlimited variety of fillings!

'A nadie se le niega un taco.'
NO ONE SHOULD BE DENIED A TACO.

TACOS GOBERNADOR

CHEESY PRAWN TACOS

This recipe is originally from Sinaloa in the north of Mexico where seafood is abundant. In Mexico City, these tacos come with the addition of cheese and, of course, our famous fake guacamole. Tacos gobernador are not that old, being first served in a well-known restaurant in Mazatlan called Los Arcos, but in the City, we serve them in different styles and with different ingredients – I have seen them made with prawn and bacon, beans, fish and even fresh habaneros, but I'll share an easy recipe that everyone will love!

1 tablespoon unsalted butter
½ white or brown onion, finely diced
2 garlic cloves, finely chopped
1 poblano chilli or banana chilli, cut into strips
500 g (1 lb 2 oz) peeled raw king prawns (shrimp), roughly diced
1 teaspoon table salt
pinch of freshly ground black pepper
1 roma (plum) tomato, finely diced
2 tablespoons chipotle in adobo sauce
1 tablespoon whole egg mayonnaise
1 tablespoon sour cream
100 g (3½ oz) tasty cheese, grated
10 Tortillas de maiz (see page 228)
vegetable oil spray
Guacamole falso (see page 212), to serve
lime wedges, to serve

Melt the butter in a frying pan over medium heat, add the onion and garlic and cook, stirring, for 3–4 minutes, until the onion is soft. Add the poblano chilli strips and stir for 5 minutes until soft, then add the prawns, salt and pepper. Cook, stirring, until half the liquid in the pan has evaporated. Add the tomato, reduce the heat to low and add the chipotle in adobo sauce, mayonnaise and sour cream. Stir until all the ingredients are combined and heated through, then remove from the heat.

Divide the cheese and the prawn mixture among the tortillas and fold in half like a quesadilla.

Heat a comal or frying pan over medium heat and spray with vegetable oil. Add the folded tortillas and cook, turning occasionally, until the cheese melts.

Serve the tacos hot with guacamole falso drizzled over the top and lime wedges on the side.

TACOS DE BISTEC CON QUESO

STEAK & CHEESE TACOS

There are some tacos that are eaten only at specific times of day, and tacos de bistec con queso belong on the lunchtime menu at weekday street markets. I have a few favourites places, but they are usually good no matter where you buy them.

The secret to cooking the steaks is to use pork lard. The lively bubbling sound of the frying will get your mouth watering before you've even had your first bite.

6 x 100 g (3½ oz) beef minute steaks
355 ml (12½ fl oz) bottle Mexican beer
1 tablespoon table salt
150 g (5½ oz) pork lard
3 white onions, finely sliced
2 teaspoons Maggi seasoning
8 Tortillas de maiz (see page 228)
240 g (8½ oz) Oaxaca cheese
    or firm mozzarella, grated or shredded

To serve

Papas con cebolla (see page 111)
Guacamole falso (see page 212)
limes wedges

Combine the steaks with the beer and salt in a bowl and marinate in the fridge for 30 minutes.

Melt the lard in a frying pan over medium heat, add the onion and cook, stirring occasionally, for 10 minutes or until browned.

Shake off the excess liquid from the steaks and carefully add them the pan – cooking with lard can be dangerous as the fat can spatter, so make sure you add the steaks slowly. Cook the steaks for 3–4 minutes, then flip and cook for a further 2–3 minutes, until just cooked through. Remove the steaks from the pan and allow to cool slightly, then finely dice. Return to the frying pan, add the Maggi seasoning and cook over medium heat for 10 minutes, or until the meat is well browned.

Working in batches, warm the tortillas in a comal or large frying pan over medium heat for 1–2 minutes, until the edge of the tortillas is lightly golden. Flip the tortillas, sprinkle 30 g (1 oz) of the grated or shredded cheese over each tortilla and cook until the cheese is starting to melt.

Pile the steak into the cheesy tortillas and serve with the papas con cebolla, guacamole falso and lime wedges.

TACOS DE TINGA DE POLLO

SHREDDED CHILLI CHICKEN TACOS

As chipotle is my favourite chilli, this tinga sauce is always present in my home, and on the menu in my restaurants. Diners are always delighted with the flavour and the smoky taste that the adobo brings, as well as the funky colour and the perfect amount of spiciness. Some like to add sour cream to reduce the heat and, even though this is not a common mix in Mexico, I have to confess that I like it.

But what I like the most about tinga is its versatility – it can be served at room temperature if you're making tostadas, or used as a topping for sopes or tacos, as here. And you can make a vegetarian version, using carrots or zucchini (courgettes) instead of chicken.

1 kg (2 lb 3 oz) skinless chicken breasts
5 bay leaves
5 white onions, finely sliced, plus 1 onion extra, cut in half
1½ tablespoons table salt
4 roma (plum) tomatoes, roughly chopped
100 g (3½ oz) chipotles in adobo sauce
1 garlic clove
2 tablespoons vegetable oil
12 Tortillas de maiz (see page 228)

Place the chicken, bay leaves, 1 onion half and half the salt in a large saucepan and add enough water to cover. Bring to the boil over medium heat, then reduce the heat to a simmer and cook for 15 minutes or until the chicken is just cooked through. Remove the chicken from the cooking liquid and set aside to cool slightly, reserving the liquid. When the chicken is cool enough to handle, shred it with your fingers or two forks.

Using a blender, blend the tomatoes, chipotles, garlic, remaining onion half, 100 ml (3½ fl oz) of the chicken cooking liquid and the remaining salt.

Heat the vegetable oil in a large saucepan over medium heat and sauté the sliced onion for about 10 minutes or until lightly coloured. Add the tomato chipotle sauce and cook, stirring constantly, for about 10 minutes or until the sauce darkens in colour. Add the chicken and cook, stirring frequently, for about 20 minutes or until the mixture is reduced and thick.

Serve the tinga in the tortillas.

TACOS DE
BISTEC
CON QUESO
PAGE 68

TACOS
DE TINGA
DE POLLO
PAGE 69

TACOS DE TRIPA

TRIPE TACOS

I promise you, these are unbelievably delicious – crispy and juicy – and the best place to eat them is definitely Mexico City. But I understand the name ('tripa' are beef intestines) might not be attractive until you've tried them.

I confess I didn't eat tripa until I was old enough to be brave and enjoy the traditions of my culture. I could never have become a chef by not trying foods from my own country. Nowadays I make tacos de tripa at home just for me and my son and it is by far his favourite filling.

The secret is to fry the tripe after it is nicely cooked – we like it crispy instead of chewy. Beef tripe is usually sold super-clean and ready to go, either frozen or fresh, and you get to pick either thin or thick. I personally prefer the thick variety – it's more meaty and easier to cook.

1 kg (2 lb 3 oz) beef tripe
juice of 5 limes
1 white onion, cut in half
10 bay leaves
1 tablespoon dried thyme
1 tablespoon table salt
8 garlic cloves
80 ml (⅓ cup) vegetable oil or pork lard

To serve

12 Tortillas de maiz (see page 228)
bunch of coriander (cilantro), leaves
  finely chopped
1 white onion, finely diced
Salsa verde de chile asado (see page 209)
limes wedges

Wash the tripe at least three times inside and out, but do not remove all the fat as this is where the flavour lives. Place the tripe in a bowl, pour over the lime juice and set aside in the fridge for 1 hour.

Add the tripe to a large saucepan with the onion, bay leaves, thyme, salt, garlic and 3 litres (3 qts) of water. Bring to the boil over high heat, then reduce the heat to medium–low and simmer, covered, for about 2 hours, until the tripe is soft when pierced with a knife.

Heat the oil or pork lard in a large frying pan over medium heat, add the tripe and cook for 5–7 minutes, until crispy. Remove the tripe from the pan and allow to cool slightly, then chop into 2 cm (¾ in) dice.

Pile the tripe into the tortillas and serve, topped with the coriander, onion and salsa verde de chile asado, with lime wedges on the side.

TACOS DE CARNE ENCHILADA

CHILLI PORK TACOS

I miss my Monday late lunch at the street market in Cuitlahuac Avenue, with the delicious habanero sauce. I used to go there almost every week when I was in high school. It was on my journey home, and the smell coming out of the market would catch my attention and make me walk through. Tacos de carne enchilada were my number one option. The colourful stools, the plastic flowery tablecloths, the salsa containers all along the edge of the stall to help yourself to and top up your tacos, and the large comal cooking the meat – it all added up to the perfect scenario for a hungry teenager.

1 kg (2 lb 3 oz) pork minute steaks
1 tablespoon table salt
6 dried guajillo chillies, stems removed and deveined
3 dried chiles de árbol, stems removed and deveined
2 dried ancho chillies, stems removed and deveined
1 white onion, cut in half
2 garlic cloves
2 bay leaves
1 teaspoon dried thyme
1 teaspoon dried Mexican oregano
5 whole black peppercorns
pinch of ground cinnamon
80 ml (⅓ cup) white vinegar
80 ml (⅓ cup) vegetable oil or pork lard

To serve

12 Tortillas de maiz (see page 228)
1 white onion, finely diced
chopped coriander (cilantro) leaves
Salsa de habanero con mango (see page 221)
lime wedges

Place the steaks in a bowl and add a pinch of salt to each of them. Set aside.

Heat the chillies and 250 ml (1 cup) of water in a saucepan over medium heat for 5 minutes. Add the onion, garlic, bay leaves, thyme, oregano and peppercorns, cover with a lid and reduce the heat to a gentle simmer for 3 minutes, for the flavours to infuse. Remove the pan from the heat and allow to cool slightly, then transfer the mixture to a blender with the remaining salt, the cinnamon, vinegar and 150 ml (5 fl oz) of water. Blend to a thick sauce, then pour the sauce over the steaks and marinate in the fridge for at least 45 minutes.

Heat the oil or pork lard in a comal or frying pan over medium heat. Working in batches if necessary, cook the steaks for about 3 minutes each side or until just cooked through. Allow to cool slightly, then cut the steaks into 5 mm (¼ in) dice. Heat the comal or frying pan again over medium heat, add the diced steak and cook, stirring, for 5 minutes or until tender and juicy.

Pile the steak into tortillas and serve, topped with the onion, coriander and salsa de habanero con mango, with lime wedges on the side.

MIXIOTES

STEAMED LAMB POCKETS

If we were to talk about ancestral Mexican dishes, mixiotes would be in the top ten. The Nuahuatl word means both the paper-like wrap from precious maguey leaves, and the dish that's made by wrapping and steaming meat in this parchment wrap. Even with all the preparation changes, new techniques of cooking, utensils and so on, these tender and delightfully coloured pockets of chicken or lamb meat are still found in every market.

Every time I go back to Mexico, I enjoy these at the Thursday street market in Claveria, the suburb where I grew up and where I think the best mixiotes are served.

10 dried guajillo chillies, stems removed
  and deveined
2 dried ancho chillies, stems removed
2 dried morita chillies, stems removed
3 bay leaves
5 garlic cloves
1 tablespoon table salt
1 teaspoon dried Mexican oregano
1 teaspoon dried thyme
1 teaspoon ground cumin
1 teaspoon freshly ground black pepper
1 teaspoon ground cloves
1½ tablespoons white vinegar
400 g (14 oz) boneless lamb shoulder,
  cut into 5 cm (2 in) pieces, excess fat trimmed
400 g (14 oz) boneless lamb leg, cut into 5 cm
  (2 in) pieces, excess fat trimmed

Pickled red onion

2 red onions, finely sliced
1 tablespoon white vinegar
1 teaspoon dried Mexican oregano
pinch of table salt

To serve

12 Tortillas de maiz (see page 228)
lime wedges
Salsa de habanero con zanahoria
  (see page 220)

To make the pickled red onion, bring 300 ml (10 fl oz) of water to the boil in a small saucepan, add the onion and boil for 3 minutes. Drain and transfer the onion to a small bowl. Add the vinegar, oregano and salt. Stir well, then cover and place in the fridge for 3–4 hours to pickle.

Heat the chillies, bay leaves and 500 ml (2 cups) of water in a saucepan over medium heat, bring to the boil, then reduce the heat to a simmer and cook for 5 minutes. Remove the chillies using a slotted spoon and set aside to cool. Transfer the chillies to a blender with the garlic, salt, oregano, thyme, cumin, pepper, cloves, vinegar and 200 ml (7 fl oz) of the chilli cooking water and blitz to a thick sauce.

Place the lamb in a large non-reactive bowl and add the sauce. Toss to combine, then set aside in the fridge to marinate overnight.

The next day, evenly divide the lamb and sauce among six 20 cm (8 in) squares of foil. Bring the edges together to make small foil packets and secure with kitchen string. Transfer the foil packets to a large steamer set over a saucepan of simmering water. Cover the steamer with a large tea towel, seal with the lid and steam for 2 hours or until the lamb is tender. (Check the water level in the pan every 30 minutes and top it up when necessary.)

Serve the mixiotes with the tortillas, pickled red onion, lime wedges and salsa de habanero con zanahoria. Enjoy!

AZCAPOTZALCO!
AZCAPOTZALCO!
AZCAPOTZALCO!
AZCAPOTZALCO!
AZCAPOTZALCO!
AZCAPOTZALCO!
AZCAPOTZALCO!

(THE PLACE WHERE
I AM FROM)

AZCAPOTZALCO IS A BOROUGH IN THE NORTHWEST OF MEXICO CITY, AND TAKES ITS NAME FROM THE NAHUATL WORD 'AZCAPOTZALLI' (ANTHILL) PLUS 'CO' (PLACE).

So, the place of anthills, or just the place of ants. This is where I was raised and lived for 25 years before coming to Australia. I have deep memories of my childhood, having all my family together, giving birth to my son, my first friends, first love, moving houses, my first dog! But my favourite legend about my beloved Azcapotzalco is the one about corn.

This Aztec myth is the story of the god Quetzalcoatl – the feathered serpent – promising his people they would never suffer hunger. But they were growing weak from feeding only on roots and plants, so he needed to bring the unreachable golden seed from the top of the mountains to feed them. Quetzalcoatl transformed himself into a black ant and, with the help of a red ant, reached the top of the mountain. He carried the corn grain down for the Aztecs to cultivate and harvest.

Today, corn is the most important ingredient of the Mexican diet – consumed in its natural way or transformed into masa to be baked into tortillas, totopos, champurrado, tamales, sopes, gorditas, petroleras, quesadillas, enchiladas, tacos and so many other foods that form the endless Mexican gastronomy.

The red ant that helped Quetzalcoatl is painted on the wall of the Azcapotzalco Cathedral. The myth tells that the wall magically grows a little every year and the end of the world will come when the red ant reaches the top of the wall. This marvellous cathedral also holds part of our Mexican independence history from the last battles against the Spanish in 1821.

Who are the chinotolos? Well, that's the name of the Azcapotzalco population, and it comes from the ant having a large rear, which lets it carry heavy items for a long time. In the same way, the people are represented as strong, hard workers after Quetzalcoatl gave them the golden seed. My favourite tattoo is the feathered serpent Quetzalcoatl drawn on my back, to represent my homeplace and the importance of this god in our Mexican culture, traditions and gastronomy.

TACOS DE PICADILLO

GROUND BEEF TACOS

I used to make quesadillas de picadillo in Sydney back in 2015 when I started doing the markets, and they were incredibly popular. I always wondered where the idea for chili con carne came from and I now think that a combination of ground beef picadillo and frijoles charros might be what inspired the popular Tex-Mex dish. Tacos de picadillo are very popular among the 'tacos de guisado' with their delicious stewed fillings.

5 roma (plum) tomatoes, cut into chunks
2 carrots, cut into 1 cm (½ in) dice
2 potatoes, cut into 1 cm (½ in) dice
2 tablespoons vegetable oil
2 garlic cloves
1 white onion, finely diced, plus ½ onion extra, roughly chopped
500 g (1 lb 2 oz) minced (ground) beef
1 tablespoon table salt
1 teaspoon freshly ground black pepper
1 sweetcorn cob, husks and silks removed, kernels stripped
100 g (3½ oz) green beans, trimmed and sliced
2 bay leaves

To serve

Arroz Mexicano (see page 237)
8 Tortillas de maiz (see page 228)
Jalapenos toreados (see page 238)

Place the tomato and 500 ml (2 cups) of water in a saucepan and bring to the boil over medium heat. Cook for 10 minutes or until soft, then remove using a slotted spoon and set aside to cool. Add the carrot and potato to the water and cook for 10 minutes, until soft, then strain the liquid, reserving 250 ml (1 cup). Allow the carrot and potato to cool.

Heat the vegetable oil in a frying pan over medium heat, add one garlic clove and cook until slightly burnt (this adds a bitter edge to the sauce), then remove and discard. Add the finely diced onion to the pan and saute for 5 minutes or until softened. Add the beef and salt, breaking up the mince with the back of a wooden spoon, then reduce the heat to low and cook for 10 minutes or until the beef is cooked through.

Place the cooked tomato, remaining garlic clove, extra chopped onion, black pepper and reserved cooking water in a blender and blend until smooth. Pour the sauce over the cooked mince and add the corn kernels, green beans, bay leaves, carrot and potato. Cook, stirring occasionally, for 10 minutes or until thickened slightly. Remove and discard the bay leaves.

Spoon a little rice into the tortillas, top with picadillo and serve with a side of jalapenos toreados.

TACOS DE ROPA VIEJA

'OLD CLOTHES' TACOS

The name 'ropa vieja' means, quite literally, 'old clothes'. It comes from the story of a man who was very poor and didn't have enough money to buy food for his family. Desperate, he sold his old clothes to get these ingredients. This dish took off in Mexico after Cuban immigrants had arrived and brought a bit of their own gastronomy to mix with ours. Even though ropa vieja exists all over the country, it's not common outside Mexico City, where this special dish is used as a topping for our famous tacos de guisado menu.

My grandma was a lover of ropa vieja, and it was usual for us to have it at home. I feel somehow sad when I ask my Mexican friends about it and they don't even remember or recognise the name. How can you forget such a funky name?

500 g (1 lb 2 oz) flank or skirt steaks
1 white onion, finely chopped,
   plus 1 onion extra, halved
5 bay leaves
1 teaspoon table salt
3 cloves
80 ml (⅓ cup) olive oil
1 green bell pepper (capsicum), julienned
1 yellow bell pepper (capsicum), julienned
1 red bell pepper (capsicum), julienned
2 garlic cloves, crushed
5 roma (plum) tomatoes, roughly chopped
1 dried chile de árbol, stem removed
100 ml (3½ fl oz) tomato passata
   (pureed tomatoes)
1 tablespoon dried Mexican oregano
1 teaspoon ground cumin
1 teaspoon freshly ground black pepper
pinch of paprika
3 tablespoons white wine

To serve

12 Tortillas de maiz (see page 228)
Arroz Mexicano (see page 237)
Salsa de siete chiles (see page 217)

Place the steaks, 1 onion half, the bay leaves, half the salt, cloves and 1 litre (34 fl oz) of water in a large saucepan over medium heat. Bring to the boil, then reduce the heat to a simmer and cook for 1 hour or until the steak is tender. Strain the stock into a bowl, set the steaks aside and discard the remaining solids. Finely shred the steak with your fingers or two forks and reserve.

Heat the olive oil in a large frying pan over medium heat and saute the finely chopped onion, bell peppers and garlic for 8–10 minutes, until softened.

Place the tomato, chile de árbol, remaining onion half, tomato passata, oregano, cumin, black pepper, paprika, remaining salt, wine and 200 ml (7 fl oz) of the reserved cooking water in a blender and blend until combined, but still slightly chunky. Add it to the pan with the onion and bell peppers and cook for 5 minutes or until the colour darkens slightly. Add the shredded steak, then reduce the heat to low and cook, stirring occasionally, for about 20 minutes, until thickened.

Pile the steak filling onto tortillas, along with some rice and salsa, and serve.

TACOS
DE PICADILLO
PAGE 98

TACOS DE
ROPA VIEJA
PAGE 99

TACOS DE RAJAS CON CREMA

SLICED CHILLI & CREAM TACOS

Poblano peppers originate from Puebla, but you can now find them at any mercado, supermarket, tianguis (open-air market) or grocery shop all year round in Mexico City. I feel very excited if ever I go to the supermarket in Sydney and find fresh poblanos! The flavour takes me back to Mexico with the first bite.

We have many recipes that use poblanos, and this is the most popular one for tacos, being an excellent vegetarian option. The chillies can be hot, depending on the season, so adding cream to this dish is the perfect solution for neutralising any spiciness.

5 poblano chillies, fresh or tinned
2 tablespoons unsalted butter
1 white onion, finely sliced
1 garlic clove, crushed
2 sweetcorn cobs, husks and silks removed, kernels stripped
1 teaspoon table salt
250 g (1 cup) sour cream
1 teaspoon ground white pepper
8 Tortillas de maiz (see page 228)
Arroz Mexicano (see page 237), to serve

If you are using fresh chillies, heat a barbecue grill or gas flame on the stove and place the chillies on the barbecue or directly on the gas flame. Cook, turning the chillies frequently, until slightly burnt on all sides and soft without any shiny skin remaining. Transfer to a large zip-lock bag while hot and set aside to sweat for 10 minutes.

Peel the blackened skins from the chillies and discard, along with the stems and seeds. If you are using tinned chillies, drain and remove the stems and the seeds. Slice the chillies lengthways into strips 5 mm (¼ in) thick.

Melt the butter in a large frying pan over low heat, add the onion and garlic and cook for about 5 minutes, until the onion is soft. Add the chilli, corn kernels, salt, most of the sour cream and the white pepper, and cook, stirring, for about 5 minutes or until heated through.

Serve the chilli mixture on warmed tortillas with arroz Mexicano, with the remaining sour cream drizzled over the top.

TACOS DE TINGA RES

SHREDDED CHILLI BEEF TACOS

Tinga de res is more commonly enjoyed as a topping on night-time tostadas eaten especially at Independence Day Celebrations in Mexico City. Each recipe might be slightly different depending on who is making it, and you might also find it served in tortas, quesadillas, gorditas or burritos. No matter how it's presented, tinga de res, with its unique pasilla chilli flavour, is the best to satisfy any antojito (snack) craving.

We used to serve tinga de res in my dad's restaurant, El Cuervo, back in 2010 in Sydney, and it was one of his bestsellers – the tender meat and juicy chilli combination was the star of our lunch burritos!

1 kg (2 lb 3 oz) chuck steak, cut into
   5 cm (2 in) pieces
1 white onion, finely sliced, plus ½ onion extra
3 dried pasilla chillies
2 dried cascabel chillies
5 bay leaves
1 tablespoon table salt
2 roma (plum) tomatoes, roughly chopped
1 teaspoon freshly ground black pepper
2 tablespoons vegetable oil
12 Tortillas de maiz (see page 228)
Arroz Mexicano (see page 237), to serve

Place the steak, the onion half, the chillies, bay leaves and salt in a saucepan. Add enough water to cover the mixture and bring to the boil over medium heat. Cook for about 1 hour, until the steak is tender, then remove using a slotted spoon and set aside to cool. Strain the cooking water into a bowl and reserve the solids.

Shred the steak using your hands or two forks. Remove the stems from the chillies and place the chillies in a blender with the boiled onion, 300 ml (10 fl oz) of the cooking water, the tomato and black pepper. Blend until smooth, then strain into a bowl to remove any solids.

Heat the oil in a large saucepan over medium heat, add the sliced onion and saute for about 5 minutes, until soft. Add the chilli sauce and cook, stirring occasionally, for about 10 minutes, until slightly darker in colour. Add the shredded steak and cook, stirring, for about 10 minutes, until heated through and well combined.

Serve the tinga de res on warm tortillas with arroz Mexicano.

TACOS DE PAPAS CON CHORIZO

POTATO & CHORIZO TACOS

This recipe reminds me of primary school 'kermesses' (carnivals) when the parents would organise stalls with different games, activities and, of course, food. Papas con chorizo are affordable and bulky, easy for kids to eat and enjoyable for all ages. I can't believe that something so simple can be so delicious and now I realise how much I miss it!

This is my friend Juan Manuel's favourite dish and I usually have it available for whenever he has a craving. You can serve it as a topping for a taco, sope or tostada.

500 g (1 lb 2 oz) potato, cut into 4 mm (¼ in) dice
2 tablespoons pork lard
1 large white onion, diced
pinch of sweet paprika

Chorizo

2 dried guajillo chillies
2 bay leaves
1 teaspoon table salt
½ teaspoon ground cumin
½ teaspoon dried Mexican oregano
½ teaspoon ground cloves
1 teaspoon crushed garlic
½ teaspoon ground coriander
1 teaspoon freshly ground black pepper
pinch of ground cinnamon
1¾ tablespoons white vinegar
3 teaspoons white tequila
350 g (12½ oz) minced (ground) pork
50 g (1¾ oz) pork lard

To serve

8 Tortillas de maiz (see page 228)
Guacamole falso (see page 212)

To make chorizo, place the guajillo chillies and bay leaves in a small saucepan, cover with cold water and bring to the boil over high heat. Simmer for 5 minutes or until the chilli is soft. Strain, reserving the cooking water, and allow the chillies to cool. Discard the bay leaves.

Place the chillies, salt, cumin, oregano, cloves, garlic, coriander, pepper, cinnamon, vinegar, tequila and 2½ tablespoons of the chilli cooking water in a blender and blend until smooth.

Place the pork and lard in a non-reactive bowl and add the chilli mixture, mixing it through the meat with your hands until well combined. Cover and leave to marinate overnight in the fridge.

The next day, place the potato in a saucepan and cover with cold water. Bring to the boil over high heat, then reduce the heat to medium and simmer for 10 minutes or until just tender. Drain.

Heat a comal or heavy-based frying pan over medium heat, add the marinated pork and cook, stirring occasionally, for 15–20 minutes, until tender and crisp.

Heat the pork lard in a frying pan over medium heat, add the onion and cook for about 7 minutes or until slightly burnt and crisp. Add the potato, chorizo and paprika and cook, stirring occasionally, for about 5 minutes or until heated through.

Pile the potato and chorizo mixture onto tortillas and serve with the guacamole falso.

TACOS DE PAPAS CON CEBOLLA

POTATO AND ONION TACOS

My friend Lulu used to have this on her table at lunchtime. I remember putting it into my tacos – the spicy flavour with fresh chilli and the potato made it truly delicious. It's a very common filling at street stalls where it's often available as a complimentary topping.

It's one of my favourites. You can use it for any occasion, serve it by itself or add to tacos, use as a topping for bread or just put it on the table with snacks and let your guests decide!

Here I use green jalapeno, serrano or Thai chillies, but you can also use poblano chillies to give extra flavour.

1 kg (2 lb 3 oz) potatoes, cut into 5 mm (¼ in) dice
2 tablespoons vegetable oil
1 white or brown onion, finely sliced
5 green jalapeno, serrano or Thai chillies, sliced
1 teaspoon table salt
pinch of black pepper

To serve

8 Tortillas de maiz (see page 228) or sliced
    white bread (optional)
Valentina hot sauce
lime wedges

Place the potato in a large saucepan, cover with cold water and bring to the boil over high heat. Reduce the heat slightly and simmer the potato for about 10 minutes, until just cooked through. Drain.

Heat the oil in a frying pan over medium heat, add the onion and saute for about 7 minutes, until lightly browned. Add the chilli and cook, stirring frequently, for 3–4 minutes, until soft, then add the potato, salt and pepper, stir and lightly mash the potato, leaving some diced and some mashed. (I hope this makes sense!)

Serve hot or cold in a tortilla or bread slice, or as a side to other dishes, with a drizzle of Valentina hot sauce and lime wedges.

TIP

ADD A PINCH OF PAPRIKA IF YOU
WANT TO ADD SOME COLOUR!

There are thousands of soups made all over Mexico. Some are everyday fare for the home table; some are well-known entrees to a great meal. Others are fighting to keep themselves alive in remote towns, where the indigenous people guard their secrets and techniques – I'm thinking of dishes like caldo de piedra (stone soup) from Oaxaca, which is less a soup and more an honorific representation of gratitude to women.

Soups occupy a very special place in our cuisine. They represent comfort, family love, tradition, a quick snack, medicine for fertility, and even a cure for a broken heart or hangover. From European recipes to Mexican creativity, we have seemingly endless varieties that can't be ignored. These magic potions are capable of reanimating and reviving any spirit with surprising flavours, amazing combinations, magical toppings and special presentations.

When eating pozole, for example – which can be a wild dining experience – you will often find yourself crossing arms and knocking hands with all the other diners at the table, as everyone reaches excitedly for the multitude of ingredients, toppings and condiments on offer.

Every state has its own favourite sopa. They reflect the personality and loving connection between tradition and gastronomy, sometimes using very specific local ingredients only available in that region; other times everyday ingredients or even leftovers.

SOPA DE TORTILLA

TORTILLA SOUP

Sopa de tortilla is also known as sopa Azteca and is probably the most famous, internationally known Mexican soup. It was originally from Tlaxcala state but is now found all over the country. This is what I would order every time I visited La Marquesa National Park, an hour's drive out of the city. When I came to Australia, I started making it every Sunday at the markets in Sydney and people would ask me for the recipe – so I'm sharing it here.

3 pasilla chillies, stalks, veins
  and seeds removed
1 dried ancho chilli, stalks, veins
  and seeds removed
5 roma (plum) tomatoes, roughly chopped
½ white onion, roughly chopped
2 garlic cloves
10 Tortillas de maiz (see page 228)
200 ml (7 fl oz) vegetable oil,
  plus 1 tablespoon extra
3 teaspoons table salt

To serve
2 avocados, cut into 3 cm (1¼ in) dice
100 g (3½ oz) sour cream
100 g (3½ oz) queso fresco or feta, crumbled
lime wedges

Cut one pasilla chilli into thin strips and set aside – we'll use this to garnish the soup.

Place 500 ml (2 cups) of water, the remaining pasilla chillies and the ancho chilli in a saucepan and bring to the boil. Reduce the heat to a simmer and cook for 3–5 minutes, until the chillies are soft. Strain the chillies into a bowl and reserve the chilli water. Place the chillies and 250 ml (1 cup) of the chilli cooking water, the tomato, onion and garlic in a blender and blend until smooth. Strain the liquid into a bowl. Discard the remaining chilli water.

Cut the tortillas into strips 1 cm (⅓ in) wide.

Heat the 200 ml (7 fl oz) of oil in a frying pan over medium–low heat. Lower a tortilla strip into the oil to test if the oil is hot enough. If it sizzles, then the oil is ready. Working in batches, fry the tortilla strips for 2 minutes or until crisp, then transfer to a bowl lined with paper towel to drain.

Lower the reserved pasilla chilli strips into the oil and fry for 1 minute or until crisp. Drain on paper towel.

Heat the 1 tablespoon of oil in a large saucepan over medium heat. Add the strained chilli sauce and salt and stir well, then reduce the heat to low, add 1 litre (34 fl oz) of water and gently bring to the boil. Cook for 5 minutes, then remove from the heat.

To serve, divide the fried tortilla strips among bowls and pour the soup over the top. Decorate the top of the soup with the avocado, sour cream and cheese, and finish with the fried chilli strips and a squeeze of lime juice.

PANCITA

TRIPE SOUP

Pancita has been the number one hangover cure in CDMX for years! The flavour of the chillies makes you forget that it's made with beef tripe. My dad used to adore pancita from a weekend stall that was famous in the area of Claveria; however, my favourite is definitely from La Cocina de Chayito stall in Santa María la Ribera – it never disappoints. You can also find this soup in cantinas – La Toluca, for instance, used to be my go-to place to cure myself of a hangover before drinking a black beer!

1 kg (2 lb 3 oz) beef tripe
juice of 1 lime
8 dried guajillo chillies, stalks removed
5 dried chiles de árbol, stalks removed
1 white onion, cut in half
10 garlic cloves
1 teaspoon freshly ground black pepper
1 tablespoon dried Mexican oregano
1 roma (plum) tomato, roughly chopped
1½ tablespoons table salt
2 tablespoons vegetable oil
5 bay leaves

To serve

1 white onion, diced
dried Mexican oregano
crushed dried chile de árbol or pequin chilli
lime wedges
Tortillas de maiz (see page 228)

Wash the tripe at least three times inside and out, but do not remove all the fat as this is where the flavour lives. Cut the tripe into 5 cm (2 in) pieces and place in a bowl with 1 litre (34 fl oz) of warm water. Add the lime juice and set aside for 30 minutes. Drain.

Place 500 ml (2 cups) of water, the chillies, one onion half and four garlic cloves in a saucepan. Simmer over medium–high heat for 3–5 minutes, until the chillies are soft. Strain, reserving the liquid and the solids.

Transfer the cooked chillies, onion, garlic and 125 ml (½ cup) of the chilli cooking water to a blender and add the pepper, oregano and tomato. Blend until smooth, then strain the sauce into a bowl and add 1 tablespoon of the salt. The sauce should be slightly thick.

Heat the oil in a saucepan, add the sauce and cook, stirring occasionally, for 5 minutes or until it darkens in colour.

Bring 2 litres (2 qts) of water to the boil in a large saucepan, add the tripe and the remaining onion half, garlic cloves, salt and the bay leaves. Reduce the heat to a simmer and cook for 40 minutes or until the tripe is soft and easily pierced with a knife. Fish out and discard the onion, garlic cloves and bay leaves, add the sauce and stir until heated through.

Divide the soup among bowls and serve topped with diced onion, a little oregano and crushed chilli, with lime wedges and tortillas on the side.

▲▲▲▲▲▲▲▲▲▲ ∿∿ ▲▲▲▲▲▲▲▲▲▲

SOPA DE FIDEO SECO

MEXICAN SPAGHETTI

This is one of my dad's favourite soups. We would have it on special occasions or whenever he was coming back from Australia to Mexico to visit us. This is a dish you might not always find at fondas or cocinas economicas, but fancier Mexican restaurants should have it on the menu.

Every family has their own recipe for fideo seco, but there is a flavour that unites them all and that is chipotle – my favourite chilli and the most important ingredient here.

I use short-cut angel hair pasta in this recipe, as fideo itself is not available in Sydney.

2 roma (plum) tomatoes, roughly chopped
½ small white or brown onion, roughly chopped
2 chipotle chillies in adobo sauce
½ garlic clove
2 teaspoons table salt
1 tablespoon vegetable oil
200 g (7 oz) short-cut angel hair pasta
100 g (3½ oz) queso fresco, Cotija, panela or feta, crumbled

Place the tomato, onion, chipotles, garlic, salt and 250 ml (1 cup) of water in a blender and blitz to a runny sauce.

Heat the oil in a large saucepan over low heat and add the pasta. Cook, stirring, for about 7 minutes, until the pasta is lightly toasted. Add the tomato sauce and bring the mixture to the boil, then reduce the heat to low and add 2½ tablespoons of water. Cover with a lid and cook for 10–12 minutes, until the pasta is cooked through and the sauce is mostly absorbed.

Divide the fideo seco between shallow bowls, scatter the cheese over the top and serve.

BIRRIA
GOAT SOUP

Birria is a soup from Guadalajara that has become very popular, especially in the north of Mexico where trendy quesabirria (a sort of cross between a taco and a quesadilla) are all over social media. The original recipe contains goat meat, but you can also make it with beef or lamb.

Back in Sydney, birria is one of the most popular taco fillings. I have even seen it served with noodles and in ramen – fun and exotic, but very different to how we eat it in Mexico!

1 kg (2 lb 3 oz) goat or lamb leg and ribs, leg cut into 5 cm (2 in) chunks
3 bay leaves
5 whole black peppercorns
2 whole cloves
1 white onion, finely diced
12 Tortillas de maiz (see page 228), to serve

Birria marinade

2 dried guajillo chillies, stalks removed
2 dried pasilla chillies, stalks removed
2 dried cascabel chillies, stalks removed
1 teaspoon table salt
1 tablespoon vegetable oil
2 tomatoes, roughly chopped
1 white onion, roughly chopped
1 teaspoon ancho chilli powder
1 teaspoon dried Mexican oregano
1 teaspoon crushed ginger
1 garlic clove
1 teaspoon ground cumin
330 ml (11 fl oz) bottle Mexican lager
2 tablespoons white vinegar

To make the marinade, place the chillies in a saucepan and cover with 1 litre (34 fl oz) of water. Bring to the boil, then reduce the heat to a simmer and cook for 5 minutes or until the chillies are soft. Pour the chillies and the cooking water into a blender and add the salt. Blend until smooth.

Heat the oil in a saucepan over medium heat, add the chilli mixture and cook, stirring occasionally, for 7–10 minutes, until it darkens slightly.

Add the remaining marinade ingredients to the blender and blend until smooth, then pour into a large bowl and add the chilli sauce. Taste for seasoning, then add the goat or lamb and toss well to coat. Cover with plastic wrap and marinate in the fridge overnight.

Fill the base of a steamer saucepan with about 2.5 cm (1 in) of water and add the bay leaves, peppercorns and cloves. Place the marinated meat in the steamer and steam over low heat for 8 hours or until the meat is completely tender (check regularly that there is enough water in the base of the steamer). Allow the meat to cool slightly, then shred using two forks.

Using a slotted spoon, remove and discard the bay leaves, peppercorns and cloves from the cooking water and add about 1 litre (34 fl oz) of water to dilute it. Taste, and add a little more water if the flavour is still very strong.

Divide the meat among serving bowls, pour over the diluted stock and top with the onion. Serve with the tortillas on the side.

POZOLE ROJO

PORK & HOMINY SOUP

There are three traditional styles of pozole: green, white and red, just like the Mexican flag. There's nothing more Mexican than this pork and hominy soup, and it's the favourite dish for Independence Day celebrations. My favourite is pozole verde, but there's no doubt that this red version is the most popular in the city. This delicious soup is also originally from Guadalajara, and there are other versions from Guerrero, my grandpa's hometown.

The word 'pozole' comes from the Nahuatl language and means 'boiled' or 'foam'. The hominy maize is white, round and large-grained – more puffy than regular corn. It looks like a flower when it's boiled and turns the water foamy.

500 g (1 lb 2 oz) bone-in chicken thighs
500 g (1 lb 2 oz) boneless pork shoulder, diced into large chunks
4 pork trotters
1½ tablespoons table salt
3 bay leaves
1 brown onion, cut in half
½ garlic bulb, halved crossways, plus 1 extra clove
3 dried guajillo chillies, stalks removed
2 dried ancho chillies, stalks removed
boiling water
pinch of dried Mexican oregano, plus extra to serve
2 tablespoons vegetable oil
800 g (1 lb 12 oz) tinned hominy, drained

To serve

1 iceberg lettuce, shredded
½ small white onion, diced
4 radishes, sliced
crushed chile de árbol
Tostadas (see page 233)
200 g (7 oz) sour cream
lime wedges

Fill a large stockpot with 2 litres (2 qts) of water, add the chicken, pork shoulder, trotters, 1 tablespoon of the salt, the bay leaves, one onion half and the garlic bulb. Bring to the boil, then reduce the heat to low and simmer for 1½ hours or until the meat is tender.

Meanwhile, place the chillies in a heatproof bowl and add boiling water to cover. Soak for 20 minutes or until the chillies are soft. Transfer the chillies and 100 ml (3½ fl oz) of the chilli soaking water to a blender, add the remaining onion, garlic clove, salt and the oregano, and blend until smooth. Strain the sauce into a bowl and discard any remaining solids.

Heat the oil in a large saucepan over medium heat. Add the chilli sauce and cook for about 7 minutes or until it darkens slightly.

Using a slotted spoon, remove and discard the bay leaves, onion and garlic bulb from the stockpot. Remove the meat and set aside, then add the chilli sauce and hominy to the stock. Simmer for 30 minutes or until the hominy turns slightly red.

Shred the chicken, pork and trotters with your fingers or two forks and discard the skin and bones. Return the meat to the soup and heat through.

Divide the soup among bowls and top each bowl with lettuce, onion, radish, crushed chilli and extra oregano. Serve with a side of tostadas topped with sour cream, and lime wedges.

BIRRIA
PAGE 122

POZOLE ROJO
PAGE 123

CALDO DE POLLO

CHICKEN & VEGETABLE SOUP

Caldo de pollo is considered by Mexican mothers to be the magic medicine that cures everything. My mum, grandma, aunties and cousins make this chicken broth whenever anyone in the family is feeling unwell or down in the dumps. I follow my family's nature and keep the tradition in Australia by doing the same for my son – he knows exactly what he is going to eat if I hear him coughing or sneezing!

This dish is also welcome as part of comida corrida (instead of the pasta soup), as well as being served in restaurants as a main meal with tortillas or a bread roll. The chicken broth might sound so easy that you feel there's no need for a recipe. But I haven't found a place that sells or offers anything similar to the deliciousness we have in Mexico City.

½ brown onion
5 bay leaves
2 garlic cloves
1 tablespoon table salt
1 kg (2 lb 3 oz) chicken drumsticks
150 g (5½ oz) chicken breast
1 tablespoon chicken stock powder
4 potatoes, cut into 4 cm (1½ in) pieces
4 sweetcorn cobs, husks and silks removed
2 carrots, sliced
2 celery stalks, cut into 3 cm (1¼ in) pieces
bunch of coriander (cilantro)
200 g (7 oz) Arroz Mexicano (see page 237)

To serve

Tortillas de maiz (see page 228)
sliced avocado
lime wedges

Place the onion, bay leaves and garlic in a large saucepan and cover with 3 litres (3 qts) of water. Add the salt and bring to the boil over high heat, then boil for 4 minutes.

Add the chicken drumsticks, breast and chicken stock powder, then reduce the heat to medium and cook for 15 minutes. Add the vegetables and bunch of coriander and simmer for 20 minutes or until the vegetables are tender and the chicken is cooked through.

Remove and discard the coriander. Remove the chicken breast from the pan and shred it using two forks, then return it to the pan.

Divide the soup among bowls, making sure each bowl has an even amount of chicken and vegetables. Add 2 tablespoons of arroz Mexicano and serve with tortillas, avocado and lime wedges on the side.

SOPA TARASCA

TARASCA SOUP

From the heart of Michoacán state to my beloved CDMX, sopa tarasca positions itself as one of our favourite soups. Its similarity to sopa Azteca might get you confused – they are served with the same toppings – but the difference between them is in the thickness of the soup, and, of course, the rich flavour of the pinto beans.

3 dried pasilla chillies, stalks, veins and seeds removed
1.5 litres (51 fl oz) chicken stock
1 dried ancho chilli, stalks, veins and seeds removed
11 Tortillas de maiz (see page 228)
5 roma (plum) tomatoes, cut in half
½ white onion, roughly chopped
1 tablespoon dried Mexican oregano
2 garlic cloves
200 ml (7 fl oz) vegetable oil, plus 2 tablespoons extra
1 tablespoon table salt
2 black peppercorns
2 bay leaves
100 g (3½ oz) Frijoles negros (see page 226)
1 litre (34 fl oz) bean cooking water (see page 226)

To serve
2 avocados, cut into 3 cm (1¼ in) dice
150 g (5½ oz) sour cream
150 g (5½ oz) queso fresco or feta, crumbled

Cut one pasilla chilli into thin strips and set aside – we'll use this to garnish the soup.

Place 500 ml (2 cups) of the chicken stock, the remaining pasilla chillies and the ancho chilli in a saucepan and bring to the boil. Reduce the heat to a simmer and cook for 3–5 minutes, until the chillies are soft. Add one tortilla and continue to simmer until soft, then transfer the mixture to a blender, add the tomato, onion, oregano and garlic and blend until smooth. Strain the mixture into a bowl, discarding any remaining solids.

Heat the 2 tablespoons of oil in a large saucepan over medium–high heat. Add the tomato mixture, salt, peppercorns and bay leaves and bring to the boil, then reduce the heat to a simmer and cook for 5 minutes or until the mixture darkens in colour.

Place the beans and bean cooking water in a blender and blitz until smooth, then strain the mixture into the sauce and add the remaining chicken stock. Cook for 5 minutes or until heated through, then pick out the bay leaves and peppercorns and discard.

Cut the remaining tortillas into strips 1 cm (⅓ in) wide.

Heat the oil in a frying pan over medium–low heat. Lower a tortilla strip into the oil to test if the oil is hot enough. If it sizzles, then the oil is ready. Working in batches, fry the tortilla strips for 7 minutes or until crisp, then transfer to a bowl lined with paper towel to drain.

Lower the reserved pasilla chilli strips into the oil and fry for 1 minute until crisp. Drain on paper towel.

To serve, divide the fried tortilla strips among bowls and pour the soup over the top. Finish with the avocado, sour cream, cheese and fried chilli strips, and enjoy.

SOPA AGUADA

PASTA SOUP

Apologies to any Italians who get mad when you see this recipe, but I do hope you try it! Sopa aguada is one of the most loved sopitas (noodle soups) for Mexicans – believed to cure a flu, cough, headache and even a broken heart. Being so important, it is part of the everyday comida corrida in Mexico City.

My friend Lulu makes the best sopa aguada I have ever tried and every time I ask her secret, she always says: 'It's love!' So, make sure you add lots of love to this recipe as it might just be the cure for someone at your house that needs an apapacho (hug!).

I use short-cut angel hair pasta for this recipe, but you can use spiral, alphabet, farfalle, elbows, mini penne, mini shells and so on.

2 roma (plum) tomatoes, roughly chopped
100 g (3½ fl oz) tomato passata (pureed tomatoes)
½ small white or brown onion, roughly chopped
½ garlic clove
2 teaspoons table salt
2 tablespoons vegetable oil
200 g (7 oz) short-cut angel hair pasta
   or pasta of your choice
1 large chicken stock cube, crumbled

Place the tomato, passata, onion, garlic, salt and 250 ml (1 cup) of water in a blender and blitz to a runny sauce.

Heat the oil in a large saucepan over low heat and add the pasta. Cook, stirring, for about 7 minutes, until the pasta is lightly toasted. Add the tomato sauce and increase the heat to medium, then add the chicken stock cube and 1.5 litres (51 fl oz) of water. Bring to the boil, then cover with a lid and cook for 10–12 minutes, until the pasta is fully cooked through.

Divide the soup among bowls and serve.

TIP

TO MAKE THIS SOPA MORE OF A COMPLETE MEAL, DRIZZLE CREAM OVER THE TOP AND SERVE WITH FRIJOLES NEGROS (SEE PAGE 226), TORTILLAS DE MAIZ (SEE PAGE 228) AND YOUR FAVOURITE SALSA.

COMIDA CORRIDA

'Al dolor de cabeza, el comer le endereza.'

IF THERE'S A HEADACHE, EATING WILL CURE IT.

I might describe comida corrida in English as a 'set meal' but with very affordable prices (the words mean 'affordable meal' or 'fast meal'), with a range of options for the main dish, such as chiles rellenos, enchiladas, mole, crispy tacos, milanesas, chilaquiles or flautas.

The meal is always served in the following order: soup, rice, main dish with salad, tortillas (lots of them!), complimentary salsas on the table for self-service, and dessert.

The comida corrida is usually found at mercados, fondas or cocinas economicas and is the top option for lunchtime, especially for factory or office workers looking for places to satisfy their hunger at 2.30 pm. It can also be ordered to take away in containers and eat at home.

We would have comida corrida when there wasn't time to cook. Mum worked full-time, so Grandma Tete was always in charge of us and loved to make our favourite dishes. But the rushed life of the city pushes everyone to enjoy comida corrida from time to time!

We loved our local cocina economica, where Dona Mary was in charge. This lovely lady made a lot of food – I'm always surprised now to think back on her skills – up to seven main dishes every day, plus soup, rice, horchata, tortillas and dessert.

She knew us well as we had to walk right past her shop after school – and a bunch of mums would always be lining up to get their containers of Mary's delicious dishes to feed their entire families a full meal.

If you'd like to serve a full comida corrida for your guests – and I guarantee they would enjoy it! – you'll need to make tortillas, rice, beans, salsas, horchata, pasta soup, rice pudding and one of the main dishes from this chapter.

CHILES RELLENOS

STUFFED CHILLIES

SERVES 4

This dish is labour intensive to make but one of my favourite things to eat! I love chiles rellenos – especially when I'm not in charge of making them! If you can buy fresh poblano chillies, then do so, but don't be sad if you can't find them. I used the tinned ones for years and the flavour is excellent – sometimes even better!

8 large poblano chillies (fresh or tinned)
320 g (11½ oz) queso fresco or feta,
  cut into 8 sticks
150 g (1 cup) plain (all-purpose) flour
vegetable oil, for shallow-frying
6 eggs, separated
pinch of salt
pinch of ground white pepper

Tomato salsa

6 roma (plum) tomatoes, roughly chopped
½ white onion, roughly chopped
2 teaspoons table salt
1 small garlic clove
2 tablespoons vegetable oil

To serve

Arroz Mexicano (see page 237)
Frijoles refritos (see page 227)
Tortillas de maiz (see page 228)

If you are using fresh poblano chillies, preheat a barbecue grill or use a stovetop gas flame. Char the chillies, turning occasionally, until blackened and soft. Using tongs, immediately transfer the chillies to a large zip-lock bag and leave them to sweat for 10 minutes – this will make peeling the chillies much easier.

Once the chillies are cool enough to handle, peel the skins and discard, then open the chillies lengthways and rinse off the seeds. (If you are using tinned chillies, select the biggest ones and very gently prise them open lengthways, without breaking them, and scrape away the seeds.)

For the tomato salsa, blitz the tomato, onion, salt, garlic and 400 ml (14 fl oz) of water in a blender until smooth. Heat the oil in a saucepan over medium–high heat, add the salsa and bring to the boil. Reduce the heat and simmer for 5 minutes, until the salsa changes colour. Keep warm.

Place a cheese stick in the middle of each opened chilli, then close up and secure with toothpicks. Gently roll the stuffed chillies in the flour.

Heat enough oil to half-submerge the stuffed chillies in a deep frying pan over medium heat to 180°C (350°F) on a kitchen thermometer.

Using a stand mixer with the whisk attached, beat the egg whites on high speed for 7–10 minutes, until shiny and foamy. Add the egg yolks, one at a time, beating well between each addition, then add the salt and pepper and mix until you have a foamy batter. Dip the chillies in the batter, then lower them into the pan and shallow-fry, turning occasionally, for 3–4 minutes, until golden. Drain on paper towel.

Divide the chiles rellenos among plates and spoon some salsa over the top. Serve with arroz Mexicano, frijoles refritos and tortillas.

PUERCO EN SALSA VERDE

PORK IN GREEN SAUCE

If you are lucky enough to find fresh tomatillos, well done! But make sure they are mature enough to be used – keep in mind that tomatillos can be sour and can ruin a dish if you pop them all in without checking first. I did this once – when I was very inexperienced – and my whole sauce was sour and inedible.

I love this dish with pork chunks, but it also works well with beef or chicken. As part of a comida corrida menu, it will always come with a side of rice and whole black or refried beans.

A lot of people like to boil the pork first and then add it to the sauce; however, I think that cooking the meat in the sauce allows it to absorb much more of the flavour.

1 kg (2 lb 3 oz) tomatillos (fresh or tinned)
10 green jalapeno, serrano or Thai chillies,
    stems removed
1 white onion, roughly chopped
small bunch of coriander (cilantro), roughly chopped
1 garlic clove
1 tablespoon table salt
2 tablespoons vegetable oil
500 g (1 lb 2 oz) boneless pork shoulder, cut
    into 5 cm (2 in) dice

To serve

Arroz Mexicano (see page 237)
Frijoles refritos (see page 227)

If using fresh tomatillos, remove the husks and thoroughly wash the fruit. Roughly chop the tomatillos. Place the tomatillos, chillies, onion, coriander, garlic and salt in a blender and blitz until smooth.

Heat the oil in a saucepan over medium heat, add the tomatillo sauce and pork, stir well and bring to the boil. Cover with a lid and cook for 30 minutes, then reduce the heat to low and continue to cook, covered and adding a little water if the sauce starts to dry out, for 20–30 minutes, until the pork is tender.

Serve the pork and tomatillo sauce with arroz Mexicano and frijoles refritos on the side.

ALBONDIGAS

MEATBALLS

Meatballs are universally loved, but adding the Mexican touch is something you must learn! The smoky taste is the secret I'm about to share; and chipotle chilli is the ingredient that sets this recipe apart from what you already know.

Albondigas used to be served in all cocinas economicas in CDMX, but, sadly, I struggled to find them last time I was there, probably because the high cost of ingredients is pushing them off the menus.

In some parts of the city, the meat is moulded around a peeled hard-boiled egg (like a Scotch egg), to make a meal big enough to feed workers who are always looking for the most filling options at mercados or cocinas economicas.

500 g (1 lb 2 oz) roma (plum) tomatoes, roughly chopped
50 g (1¾ oz) chipotles in adobo sauce
½ small brown onion, roughly chopped
½ garlic clove
1 teaspoon table salt
1 tablespoon vegetable oil
1 green jalapeno or serrano chilli, left whole

Albondigas

500 g (1 lb 2 oz) minced (ground) beef
300 g (10½ oz) minced (ground) pork
100 g (3½ oz) fresh or tinned tomatillos, chopped
1½ tablespoons dried breadcrumbs
2 teaspoons ground cinnamon
2 teaspoons ground cloves
2 teaspoons freshly ground black pepper
2 teaspoons table salt
2 teaspoons long-grain rice
1 egg

To serve

Arroz Mexicano (see page 237)
Frijoles refritos (see page 227)
Tortillas de maiz (see page 228)

Place the tomato, chipotles, onion, garlic and salt in a blender and blitz to a smooth sauce.

Heat the oil in a saucepan over medium heat, add the tomato and chipotle sauce and cook, stirring occasionally, for about 7 minutes, until the sauce darkens in colour. Reduce the heat to low, add the whole chilli and cover with a lid.

Meanwhile, to make the meatballs, place the ingredients in a large bowl and mix until very well combined. Roll the mixture into 30 g (1 oz) meatballs and add them to the sauce. Cover the pan with a lid and cook the meatballs and sauce, for about 30 minutes, until the meatballs are cooked through, adding a little water if the sauce thickens too much.

Divide the albondigas among bowls and serve with arroz Mexicano, frijoles refritos and warm tortillas.

PUERCO EN SALSA VERDE

PAGE 142

ALBONDIGAS
PAGE 143

ENCHILADAS VERDES

GREEN ENCHILADAS

We Mexicans have a large variety of sauces for making different enchiladas – sometimes we use red sauce, mole or green sauce. My favourites, by far, are the green enchiladas – tasty, economical, easy to make and as spicy as you like them.

I recommend you try enchiladas inside any mercado in Mexico City, but always be sure to ask how spicy they are beforehand. You might need to ask for extra sour cream!

500 g (1 lb 2 oz) chicken breasts
1 tablespoon table salt
2 bay leaves
500 g (1 lb 2 oz) fresh or tinned tomatillos
1 white onion
2 green jalapeno or serrano chillies, stems removed
1 small garlic clove
250 ml (1 cup) chicken stock
80 ml (⅓ cup) vegetable oil

To serve

12 Tortillas de maiz (see page 228)
200 ml (7 fl oz) thickened cream or sour cream
200 g (7 oz) queso fresco, Cotija or feta, crumbled
Arroz Mexicano (see page 237)
Frijoles refritos (see page 227)

Place the chicken, half the salt and the bay leaves in a saucepan and cover with cold water. Bring to the boil, then reduce the heat and simmer for 20 minutes or until just cooked through. Drain and set the chicken aside until cool enough to handle, then shred the meat with your fingers or two forks.

If you are lucky enough to find fresh tomatillos, remove the husks and thoroughly wash the fruit. Roughly chop half the onion and finely slice the other half. Set the sliced onion aside.

Place the tomatillos, roughly chopped onion, chillies, garlic, remaining salt and the stock in a blender and blitz until smooth.

Heat 2 tablespoons of the oil in a saucepan over medium heat and add the tomatillo sauce. Simmer the sauce for 10 minutes or until it darkens in colour, adding a little more water if necessary – it needs to be runny.

Heat the remaining oil in a frying pan over medium heat and cook the tortillas for 1–2 minutes each side, until pliable and starting to crisp. Using tongs, dip the tortillas in the tomatillo sauce until completely coated, then place three tortillas, half folded, on each plate. Spoon the remaining tomatillo sauce over the enchiladas and top with the cream, cheese, shredded chicken and finely sliced onion. Serve with arroz Mexicano and frijoles refritos on the side.

CARNE EN CHILE PASILLA CON PAPAS

STEAK IN PASILLA SAUCE WITH POTATOES

The pasilla chilli is the dried version of the chilaca chilli. It has a unique, strong, bitter flavour and dark colour, and one of the best ways to use it is to cook pork or beef steaks in a pasilla sauce.

Chefs and cooks have to be creative with their comidas corrida if they want to win over the lunchtime office-worker crowd, so they need interesting menus that use seasonal ingredients, fruits or vegetables. This dish is not an 'everyday' menu item, but you'll find it at least once a month as a special of the week.

4 dried pasilla chillies (about 80 g/2¾ oz), stalks removed
1 garlic clove
1 black peppercorn
80 ml (⅓ cup) vegetable oil
1 tablespoon table salt
1 chicken stock cube, crumbled
4 potatoes, cut into 3 cm (1¼ in) dice
1 white onion, finely sliced
4 x 125 g (4½ oz) beef minute steaks

To serve

Arroz Mexicano (see page 237)
Frijoles negros (see page 226)
Tortillas de maiz (see page 228)

Boil the chillies, garlic and peppercorn in 300 ml (10 fl oz) of water for 5 minutes. Remove from the heat and set aside to cool slightly, then transfer to a blender and blitz to a smooth sauce.

Heat 2 tablespoons of the oil in a large saucepan over medium heat. Add the pasilla sauce, salt and chicken stock cube, then bring to the boil and cook, stirring frequently, for 7 minutes or until the sauce darkens in colour. Add the potato and cook for 10 minutes.

Meanwhile, heat the remaining oil in a frying pan over medium heat. Add the onion in a single layer and place the minute steaks on top. Cook, occasionally turning the steaks, for 4–5 minutes, until the steaks are just cooked through, then add the onion and steaks to the pasilla sauce, reduce the heat to low and cook for 20 minutes or until the potato is tender.

Divide the steak, potato and pasilla sauce among plates, and serve with arroz Mexicano, frijoles negros and tortillas on the side.

ENFRIJOLADAS

FOLDED BEAN TORTILLAS

Beans are one of the most-loved and important ingredients of Mexican gastronomy and have been used for thousands of years. We are experts at cultivating beans, especially in the state of Veracruz. Beans are a superfood that can come in black, white, red, tan …. All are affordable, filling, super-versatile and used in many, many side dishes. But here is a recipe where beans take the starring role.

I remember eating enfrijoladas at home during tricky financial times in my family. Nowadays, having them in Sydney is a delightful trip down memory lane.

I'm using black beans for this recipe, but you can use any variety and the results will be delicious!

1 x quantity Frijoles negros (see page 226)
2 tablespoons vegetable oil
12 Tortillas de maiz (see page 228)
250 ml (1 cup) thickened cream or sour cream
250 g (9 oz) queso fresco, Cotija or feta, crumbled
finely chopped white onion, to serve
finely chopped green jalapeno or serrano chilli,
   to serve

Place the frijoles negros in a blender, add 1.5 litres (51 fl oz) of water and blend to make a smooth, runny sauce. Pour the sauce into a saucepan and set over medium–low heat. Cook, stirring constantly, for about 5 minutes, until the sauce is just coming to the boil.

Heat the oil in a frying pan over medium heat and cook the tortillas for 1–2 minutes each side, until pliable and starting to crisp. Using tongs, dip the tortillas in the bean sauce until completely coated, then place three tortillas, half folded, on each plate.

Generously spoon some of the remaining bean sauce over the top of the enfrijoladas and top with the cream and cheese. Scatter with a little white onion and green chilli, and serve.

TACOS DORADOS

CRISPY TACOS

This is the first dish that comes to my mind when I have surprise visitors – tacos dorados are quickly made with readily available ingredients, and are so delicious they never disappoint!

My personal craving for tacos dorados is ever present. The combination of crunchy fresh lettuce, cream and cheese is one of my favourites and the salsa topping makes it just perfect.

This was the first dish I cooked when I arrived in Sydney in 2009. I think my cooking journey started right there, rolling tortillas and learning the importance of using toothpicks to hold them together!

There are many ways to serve tacos dorados: you can make a runny sauce and soak the tortillas; fill them with cheese, shredded chicken, shredded beef, chicken tinga, birria, barbacoa, potatoes, refried beans … or, believe it or not, we also eat tacos dorados without any filling, and yes, they are just as delicious!

I'm using papas con cebolla here, but feel free to use any of the fillings mentioned above.

1 x quantity Papas con cebolla (see page 111)
16 Tortillas de maiz (see page 228)
vegetable oil, for deep-frying

To serve

1 iceberg lettuce, shredded
100 ml (3½ fl oz) thickened cream or sour cream
160 g (5½ oz) queso fresco, Cotija or feta, crumbled
Salsa verde de chile asado (see page 209)

Spread 2 tablespoons of the papas con cebolla on one half of each tortilla and roll them up as tightly as you can to make little cigar-looking tacos. Place the tacos next to each other in a line in groups of four and secure them with toothpicks, ensuring that the rolled edges are facing inwards. (I hope this makes sense!) It is important that the tacos are tightly secured together to avoid the oil going through them – the outside is meant to be crispy, but the filling should remain the same consistency.

Once the tacos are rolled and secured, it's time to fry them.

Heat enough oil for deep-frying in a large saucepan to 180°C (350°F) on a kitchen thermometer. Working in batches, deep-fry the tacos, flipping occasionally, for about 6 minutes, until golden and crisp. Transfer to a plate lined with paper towel to drain.

Divide the tacos dorados among plates and top with the lettuce, cream and cheese. Drizzle with a little salsa verde and serve immediately.

ENFRIJOLADAS
PAGE 150

**TACOS
DORADOS**
PAGE 151

MOLE DE CACAHUATE

PEANUT MOLE

My friend Luis shared his recipe for this peanut sauce that can be served with pork or chicken. It is my son's favourite dish – he tried it for the first time at one of our family reunions, and shocked everyone by going back for four more helpings! It's not surprising – this dish is deliciously addictive!

500 g (1 lb 2 oz) boneless pork shoulder, cut into 5 cm (2 in) dice
1 white onion, cut in half
5 bay leaves
2 tablespoons table salt
250 g (9 oz) roma (plum) tomatoes, roughly chopped
1 garlic clove
3 tablespoons vegetable oil
300 g (10½ oz) unsalted raw peanuts
5 dried chile de árbol, stems removed
35 g (⅓ cup) dried breadcrumbs
pinch of sweet paprika

To serve
chile de árbol flakes (optional)
Arroz Mexicano (see page 237)
Tortillas de maiz (see page 228)

Place the pork, one onion half, the bay leaves and 1 tablespoon of the salt in a saucepan. Cover with about 2 litres (2 qts) of water, then bring to the boil over medium heat. Reduce the heat to medium–low and simmer for about 45 minutes, until the pork is tender. Strain the pork and reserve the stock. Discard the onion.

Place a comal or heavy-based frying pan over medium–high heat and add the tomato, remaining onion half, garlic clove and 1 tablespoon of the oil. Cook for about 7 minutes, until the tomato is slightly reduced, then transfer the mixture to a blender, along with the remaining salt, the peanuts, chillies, breadcrumbs and paprika. Blitz for 1–2 minutes, until you have a mostly smooth sauce, adding a little of the reserved pork stock, if necessary, to get the mixture moving.

Heat the remaining oil in a saucepan over medium heat, add the mole sauce and stir well, then add enough of the reserved pork stock (up to 1 litre/ 34 fl oz) to make a thick sauce. Add the pork and cook, stirring occasionally, for 15 minutes for the flavours to develop.

Sprinkle the mole with a few chile de árbol flakes, if desired, and serve with arroz Mexicano and tortillas.

CARNE A LA TAMPIQUENA

TAMPICO-STYLE STEAK

SERVES 4

SERVES 4

Tampico is a city in the north of Mexico, where meat is the first choice for the local population and is claimed to be the best in the country. Even though this looks like a big complex dish, all the recipes are already in this book and we are just going to put them together with a nice steak!

Every item on this plate represents a bit of Tampico: the beans reflect the fertility of the land; enchiladas are the lush green surroundings; cheese represents the purity of its people; guacamole is the fruit growing throughout the region; and the steak is the Pánuco River. It is usually served in an oval dish representing the shape of La Huasteca region.

My dad used to serve this at his restaurant in Sydney and it was always the most popular dish. I wonder if our guests knew its cultural importance ...?

4 x 250–300 g (9–10½ oz) beef rump steaks, fat trimmed
1 x quantity Frijoles refritos (see page 227)
1 x quantity Guacamole (see page 213)
12 Enchiladas verdes (see page 146)
80 g (2¾ oz) queso fresco, Cotija or feta, crumbled
table salt and freshly ground black pepper
vegetable oil, for drizzling
Arroz Mexicano, to serve (see page 237)
lime wedges, to serve

Make sure you have all the components ready to go before you start cooking the steaks. Arrange the frijoles refritos, guacamole, enchiladas verdes and cheese on a serving platter, ensuring that you leave enough space for the steaks.

Season the steaks with salt and pepper and drizzle with oil. Heat a chargrill pan over high heat. Working in batches, if necessary, add the steaks to the pan and cook for 1–2 minutes each side, until char lines appear and the steaks are cooked through. Transfer the steaks to the serving platter and serve with arroz Mexicano and lime wedges on the side.

ENSALADA PARA COMIDA CORRIDA

SALAD FOR COMIDA CORRIDA

This fresh crunchy salad of mixed veggies is a fundamental part of the comida corrida meal, served either as a side or on a plate by itself. In fact, you can't have a comida corrida without it.

Some interpretations are elaborate or made with roasted vegetables, but this is the classic that you will find at any mercado. It perfectly captures the authenticity of the food we eat in beautiful Mexico City.

1 iceberg lettuce, shredded
2 roma (plum) tomatoes, finely sliced
1 avocado, sliced
1 short cucumber, sliced
½ red onion, finely sliced
1 tablespoon olive oil
lime wedges, to serve

Place all the ingredients except the lime wedges in a large salad bowl and toss to combine. Serve as a side for any comida corrida, with lime wedges for squeezing over.

ENSALADA DE NOPALES

CACTUS SALAD

It's no secret that we eat cactus pretty much every day in Mexico. This salad is one of the most popular in Mexico City, and it's often complimentary when you buy street-style tacos or tlayudas, or served as a side with a main meal. You can also find different varieties of ensalada de nopales at any mercado, where big bowls of them are available for easy purchase by weight or container.

There are a few combinations of ensalada de nopales that I want to share with you, so I've included some optional additions in the ingredients list for you to play around with and pick your favourite!

1 x 800 g (1 lb 12 oz) jar pickled nopales, drained and rinsed
1 white onion, finely sliced
4 dried chiles de árbol, stems removed, finely chopped
handful of coriander (cilantro) leaves, finely chopped
2 roma (plum) tomatoes, sliced

Optional additions
finely diced avocado
crumbled queso fresco
chickpeas (garbanzo beans)
sliced dried guajillo chilli
finely sliced red onion
sweetcorn kernels
finely diced yellow habanero chilli

Place the nopales in a large salad bowl and add the remaining ingredients, along with any optional additions. Toss to combine and serve.

ENSALADA
PARA COMIDA
CORRIDA
PAGE 160

ENSALADA
DE NOPALES
PAGE 161

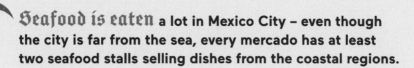

Seafood is eaten a lot in Mexico City – even though the city is far from the sea, every mercado has at least two seafood stalls selling dishes from the coastal regions.

In one of the most popular mercados in the city – in Coyoacan – the tostadas de marisco stalls are huge and the enormous range of dishes is not helpful when you're trying to choose what to eat! Some dishes might look similar, but they tend to have a secret ingredient or combination that makes each recipe, somehow, special.

For us chilangos, visits to Acapulco beach were a must. I spent a lot of weekends over there and eating fresh seafood was always one of the highlights ... caldo de camaron (prawn soup), fish tamales, pescado a la talla (fish cooked over coals), pescadillas (deep-fried fish quesadillas) and many more dishes were on my wish list before I even arrived!

But my best seafood experiences have been in Veracruz – 'porque solo Veracruz es bello!' (because only Veracruz is beautiful!). The fishing boats arrive back in port in the early morning with all their fresh seafood to sell. You can buy the famous volovanes (Veracruz-style empanadas) from the comfort of your car at a traffic-light stop, or go to 'the canteen' to buy camaron para pelar (shrimp to peel) or ostiones (oysters). Whether you go to fancy restaurants or eat at the local mercados, Veracruz has a huge variety of seafood.

NEAR THE SEA LIFE IS BETTER

'En el mar la vida es mas sabrosa.'

AGUACHILE

CHILLI PRAWNS

Aguachile is one of Mexico's most popular seafood dishes, and the original version contained just three ingredients: shrimp, water and chiltepin chilli. This is the Mexico City recipe, which has a few more inclusions – you could also add Worcestershire sauce and clamato juice. The best way to present aguachile is in a molcajete (see page 211), which is how it's famously served in the western coastal state of Sinaloa.

Chiltepin chillies are not easy to find, so I've used habaneros here. You could also use árbol, piquin or any Caribbean chilli.

1 kg (2 lb 3 oz) raw small prawns (shrimp), peeled and deveined
1 red onion, finely sliced
1 teaspoon table salt
pinch of freshly ground black pepper
2 short cucumbers, finely chopped, plus 1 short cucumber extra, roughly chopped
juice of ½ lime
3 green habanero chillies, stalks removed
small bunch of coriander (cilantro), finely chopped
2 avocados, sliced
salted crackers or Totopos (see page 232), to serve

Using a small knife, cut halfway through the back of each prawn lengthways and open it out like a butterfly. Transfer to a large non-reactive bowl and add the onion, salt, pepper and finely chopped cucumber.

Place the lime juice, habanero chilli, coriander and roughly chopped cucumber in a blender and blend until smooth. Pour the mixture over the prawns and stir to combine. Set aside in the fridge for 30 minutes for the flavours to come together.

Serve the aguachile in a bowl or a mortar and pestle for guests to help themselves, with the avocado and crackers or totopos on the side. Make sure you have a cold beer on hand to enjoy it!

CAMARONES A LA DIABLA

DEVILLED SHRIMP

Devilled shrimp is all about that red chilli sauce! It's packed with flavour and surprisingly quick and simple to make. I would eat camarones a la diabla every time I visited Acapulco, the chilango's favourite beach (or maybe just the closest!). In summertime, there was nothing better than to drive down there with family and friends.

The beaches in Mexico are fantastic: the seawater is always warm and the customer service is something I truly miss. There are food vendors walking along the beach offering delicious homemade dishes, desserts and drinks, or to braid your hair!

1 kg (2 lb 3 oz) raw prawns (shrimp), peeled and deveined, tails left intact and shells reserved
1 white onion, cut in half, half finely sliced
8 garlic cloves, crushed, plus 2 garlic cloves extra, peeled
1 teaspoon table salt
2 dried guajillo chillies
2 dried ancho chillies
5 dried chiles de árbol
3 chipotle chillies in adobo sauce
125 ml (½ cup) vegetable oil
2 large roma (plum) tomatoes, cut into large chunks
180 ml (¾ cup) tomato ketchup
freshly ground black pepper
50 g (1¾ oz) unsalted butter
Arroz Mexicano, to serve (see page 237)

Place the prawn shells, the unsliced onion, one peeled garlic clove, the salt and 250 ml (1 cup) of water in a saucepan and bring to the boil. Immediately remove from the heat and strain the stock into a bowl. Discard the solids.

Remove the stalks from all the chillies and devein and deseed the guajillo and ancho chillies (the spiciness of the sauce comes from the árbol and chipotle chillies).

Heat 2 tablespoons of the oil in a frying pan over medium heat, add the sliced onion and remaining peeled garlic clove and saute for about 4 minutes, until soft and golden. Add the tomato, stock and all the chillies, then cover and cook for 7 minutes or until the chillies are soft. Transfer the mixture to a blender and puree until smooth, then strain the sauce into a bowl. Discard any remaining solids.

Heat the remaining oil in the frying pan over medium heat. Add the pureed tomato mixture and tomato ketchup, then reduce the heat to low and cook for 5 minutes or until the sauce darkens in colour and is reduced. Season with black pepper.

Meanwhile, melt the butter in a frying pan over low heat, add the crushed garlic and stir for 2 minutes until fragrant, then add the prawns and cook for 2 minutes each side or until opaque and just cooked through. Add them to the sauce and stir to combine.

Serve the camarones a la diabla with arroz Mexicano.

PESCADO AL AJILLO

FISH WITH GARLIC & CHILLI

I feel very lucky to live in Sydney and have the fish market close to my home. Buying fresh seafood was trickier in Mexico City because the city is in a valley a long way from the ocean. I've embraced the Australian favourite fish – barramundi – and discovered the easiest way to cook a good barramundi fillet is to make it 'al ajillo', which means with garlic and guajillo chilli seasoning.

Because I usually cook with whole chillies, I get frustrated when I find small broken bits of chilli in the bottom of my shopping bag, so I decided to make good use of them. I add them to the salt shaker to make chilli salt – and magic happens!

4 x 180 g (6½ oz) skinless barramundi fillets or other firm white fish fillets
table salt and ground white pepper
3 dried guajillo chillies, stems and seeds removed, deveined
2 tablespoons olive oil
50 g (1¾ oz) unsalted butter
5 garlic cloves, finely sliced
Arroz Mexicano, to serve (see page 237)
lime wedges, to serve

Season the fish with salt and white pepper, about three pinches per fillet. Set aside.

Using scissors, cut the guajillo chilli into strips 5 mm (¼ in) wide.

Heat the olive oil and butter in a frying pan over medium heat. Add the garlic and cook, stirring, for 2 minutes, until fragrant and starting to change colour, then add the chilli and continue to cook for 3 minutes – the chilli will turn the butter and garlic orange. Using a slotted spoon, remove the garlic and chilli from the pan and reserve.

Add the fish to the pan and cook for 4–5 minutes each side until just cooked through. Return the garlic and chilli to the pan and cook for 1 minute to warm through.

Divide the fish and garlic chilli sauce among plates and serve with arroz Mexicano on the side and a few lime wedges.

PESCADO AL HORNO EN SALSA DE CHILES

BAKED CHILLI FISH

We often ate seafood at home for special occasions and during Lent. Writing down this recipe makes me realise that I don't remember eating this baked fish at any restaurant. So this is an authentic family dish taken straight from my grandma's recipe book!

My abuelita Tete would make this at Easter with my aunt Chita, who was always very kind and a true kitchen queen. I remember going with them to La Viga Market to pick the best fish at the best prices. It's the biggest seafood market in Mexico City, and eating there is a great experience that can't be missed.

5 x 180 g (6½ oz) skinless barramundi fillets or other firm white fish fillets
table salt and freshly ground black pepper
500 g (1 lb 2 oz) baby potatoes, quartered
2 dried pasilla chillies, stems and seeds removed, deveined
2 dried ancho chillies, stems and seeds removed, deveined
2 dried guajillo chillies, stems and seeds removed, deveined
2 tablespoons olive oil
100 g (3½ oz) unsalted butter
8 garlic cloves, crushed
lime wedges, to serve

Season the fish on both sides with salt and pepper. Set aside in the fridge.

Preheat the oven to 200°C (400°F).

Place the potato in a saucepan of salted water and bring to the boil over high heat. Reduce the heat to medium and simmer, uncovered, for 10–12 minutes, until just tender. Drain.

Using scissors, cut the chillies into strips 5 mm (¼ in) wide.

Heat the oil and butter in a frying pan over medium heat, stir through the garlic and add all the chilli strips. Reduce the heat to low and cook, stirring constantly, for about 2 minutes, until the chilli sweats out its colour and the butter browns. It's important to make sure the chilli doesn't burn – pasilla has a strong flavour that can turn bitter and ruin the sauce if it burns, so keep an eye on it as it cooks.

Spoon 2 tablespoons of the garlic chilli sauce into a large roasting tin, add the fish and potato, then pour the remaining sauce over the top. Cover the tin with foil, then transfer to the oven and bake for 25 minutes or until the fish is cooked through.

Serve the baked fish and potato with lime wedges on the side.

CALDO DE CAMARON

PRAWN SOUP

This popular soup is perfect for a cold-weather Sunday brunch with the family. It's also a guaranteed cure for a hangover. You will find caldo de camaron at every mercado in the Mexico City, where it is usually eaten with a bolillo (bread roll) and mayonnaise, tostadas with avocado, or just tortillas.

When I arrived in Sydney, I pushed myself to learn to make this dish exactly as I remember it from my favourite places in Mexico City: El Canto de las Sirenas and Los Jarochos. The atmosphere at these seafood restaurants was always amazing.

2 tablespoons vegetable oil
2 roma (plum) tomatoes, roughly chopped
2 dried guajillo chillies, stalks removed
1 dried ancho chilli, stalks removed
1 dried morita chilli, stalks removed
1 garlic clove
1 white onion, ½ roughly chopped,
  ½ finely chopped
1 teaspoon dried shrimp
1 teaspoon table salt
2 potatoes, cut into 3 cm (1¼ in) pieces
1 large carrot, cut into 3 cm (1¼ in) pieces
500 g (1 lb 2 oz) whole raw prawns (shrimp)
lime wedges, to serve
bolillos or crusty bread rolls, to serve (optional)

Heat 1 tablespoons of the oil in a frying pan over medium heat. Add the tomato, chillies, garlic and roughly chopped onion, and cook, stirring frequently, for 5 minutes or until the chillies are soft.

Transfer the tomato mixture to a blender and add 1 litre (34 fl oz) of water. Puree to a smooth sauce, then strain through a sieve into a bowl and discard any remaining solids.

Heat the remaining oil in a large saucepan over medium heat. Stir through the pureed sauce, dried shrimp and salt, then add the potato and carrot. Bring the mixture to the boil, then reduce the heat to medium–low and cook for 15 minutes or until the potato and carrot are soft.

Add the prawns and cook for a further 5–7 minutes, until they turn pink and are just cooked through.

Divide the caldero among bowls, ensuring that your guests receive an even quantity of prawns. Serve with the finely chopped onion sprinkled over the soup, with lime wedges and bolillos, if desired, on the side.

ATUN AL CHIPOTLE

CHIPOTLE TUNA

I remember eating tuna with chipotle during Lent when we were not allowed to eat meat. In those weeks the city would bring out its best seafood dishes to please us. This one can be mild or super-spicy – it's up to you. It is very easy to make and can be used for tacos, tortas, empanadas or tostadas. I've even served it as a finger food on mini bruschetta, with decorative sprigs of coriander on top.

2 tablespoons vegetable oil
1 large white onion, finely diced
2 roma (plum) tomatoes, finely diced
100 g (3½ oz) chipotles in adobo sauce
3 teaspoons white vinegar
500 g (1 lb 2 oz) tinned tuna chunks
   in spring water, drained
pinch of table salt
4 Tostadas (see page 233)
sprigs of coriander (cilantro), to serve

Heat the oil in a frying pan over medium heat. Add the onion and tomato and cook, stirring frequently, for 5 minutes or until soft.

Place the chipotles and vinegar in a blender and blend until smooth. Add the chilli sauce to the pan, along with the tuna and salt, and stir until just combined and heated through.

Spoon the chipotle tuna onto the tostadas, scatter with a few sprigs of coriander and serve.

MOJARRAS AL MOJO DE AJO

FRIED GARLIC FISH

SERVES 2

SERVES 2

This fried fish with garlic is my mother's favourite seafood dish, and the one she would always order whenever we were in Acapulco – we would always be shocked by how much of it she could eat! Food vendors walking along the beach are the best – they always bring exactly what you need at the right time. Mangos with chilli were also on my mum's menu – the perfect dessert after a good seafood meal!

My dad uses silver bream to make this dish in Sydney – the fish is similar to Mexican mojarra. He taught me the exact same way it's made in Mexico City, and we serve it with salad and rice. If you'd like to add a spicy kick, crush a dried guajillo chilli in the mortar and pestle with the other marinade ingredients.

2 x 300 g (10½ oz) whole silver bream
  or snapper, scaled and cleaned
8 garlic cloves
1 tablespoon table salt
5 whole black peppercorns
2 teaspoons chopped brown onion
juice of 1 lime
2 teaspoons olive oil
2 tablespoons plain (all-purpose) flour
200 ml (7 oz) vegetable oil

Mixed salad

½ iceberg lettuce, shredded
1 small roma (plum) tomato, cut into wedges
½ red onion, finely sliced
1 small avocado, cut into large dice
2 teaspoons olive oil
table salt and freshly ground black pepper

To serve

Arroz Mexicano (see page 237)
Tortillas de maiz (see page 228)
lime wedges

To make the salad, combine the ingredients in a large bowl, season with salt and pepper and set aside.

Rinse the fish under cold running water and pat dry with paper towel. Make two long slits on both sides of the body of each fish.

Using a mortar and pestle, crush the garlic, salt, peppercorns and onion. Add the lime juice and olive oil and mix well. Spread the mixture on the inside and outside of the fish, making sure you rub some into the cuts along the body. Place the fish in a baking dish and cover with plastic wrap. Set aside to marinate in the fridge for 30–60 minutes.

Sprinkle the flour on both sides of the fish, ensuring it is well covered, then shake off any excess.

Heat the vegetable oil in a large frying pan over medium heat to about 180°C (350°F) on a kitchen thermometer. Shallow-fry the fish for 5–7 minutes each side, until cooked through. Transfer to a plate lined with paper towel to drain.

Serve the fried fish with the salad, arroz Mexicano, tortillas and lime wedges.

What happens when you mix traditional Spanish ingredients with Mexican creativity?

From churros and flans to sweet bread and candied fruit, Mexico City offers thousands of options for those with a sweet tooth. There are specialist shops that focus only on desserts, while at the same time you can find lovely ladies carrying huge baskets of borrachitos or jamoncillos. Then there's the classic churros guy selling his crispy delicious doughnuts for five pesos at the bus or metro station.

Every state has its own typical sweets, such as cocadas from Veracruz, bolas de tamarindo from Acapulco, cajeta from Celaya, momias from Guanajuato, galletas de Santa Clara from Puebla and many more. The best part of being in Mexico City is that you can find all of these at every mercado – there is always a stall inside offering unique and colourful treats from all over the country. There are also the cake stalls where pastel de tres leches is always the bestseller, along with ensalada de manzana, jericallas, all kinds of jellies, arroz con leche and sometimes hand-made borrachitos.

My dad used to take us to Cuernavaca, which lies south of Mexico City, to buy fresh sweets from the producers. I enjoyed visiting these old houses where I could see the massive coppel cazos (saucepans) full of the hot sticky sugar that was being boiled and crafted into tiny pieces of heaven.

'Siempre hay un hueco pal postre!'

THERE IS ALWAYS

ROOM FOR DESSERT!

JERICALLAS

'BURNT' FLAN

This dessert is considered the 'flan from Guadalajara'. The dish has its origins in Jalisco, where it was first made by a Spanish nun, and it's now available at dessert stalls all over CDMX. There are special stalls that sell only desserts, and jericallas are always battling alongside flan (Mexican creme caramel) to be the bestseller. They are quite similar in appearance, except for the golden, slightly burnt, crust on top of jericallas.

My friend Juan Ma is obsessed with these; I was surprised to see him eating more than three a day on my last visit to Mexico! There is so much to learn about someone when you travel with them ... what I learnt is that Juan and I fought over the last jericalla in a restaurant in Tequila, Jalisco. So, I guess I'm obsessed too!

375 ml (1½ cups) full-cream (whole) milk
170 ml (⅔ cup) evaporated milk
75 g (⅓ cup) caster (superfine) sugar
1 tablespoon vanilla essence
1 cinnamon stick
2 large eggs, plus 1 egg yolk, at room
   temperature
boiling water

Combine the milk, evaporated milk, sugar, vanilla essence and cinnamon stick in a saucepan and bring to the boil over medium heat, stirring constantly to dissolve the sugar, for 5 minutes. Reduce the heat to low and cook, stirring, for 15 minutes or until slightly darkened in colour. Remove from the heat and allow to cool to room temperature for 30 minutes.

Preheat the oven to 180°C (350°F).

Whisk the eggs and egg yolk in a bowl, then whisk them into the cooled custard until completely incorporated. Strain the mixture through a sieve into a jug.

Place five 150 ml (5 fl oz) capacity glass ramekins in a deep baking dish and evenly pour the custard into the ramekins. Add enough boiling water to come halfway up the sides of the ramekins, then transfer to the oven and bake for 35 minutes, or until the jericallas are just set, with a slight wobble.

Preheat an oven grill (broiler) on medium heat. Brown the jericallas under the grill for 4–6 minutes, until dark golden and slightly burnt on the top. You can also use a kitchen blowtorch to do this.

Chill the jericallas in the fridge overnight and enjoy the next day.

PASTEL DE ELOTE

SWEETCORN CAKE

Abuelita! My grandmother is the person who comes to mind when I think of pastel de elote; she loved a slice of this delicious spongy piece of heaven. I was very lucky to walk with her, holding hands, every Thursday to our closest weekday street market in Claveria, where the main street would be closed to make way for more than 50 brightly coloured stalls in front of the mercado building.

Whenever I'm back in the city, I visit this market with my Auntie Tere. We will both become teary when we end up at Abuelita's favourite spot: the pastel de elotes and tamales stall. Gracias Tere.

My dad makes pastel de elote at one of our restaurants and I think that, every time he makes it, my grandma's presence is there with him, smelling, smiling and tasting.

500 g (3 cups) yellow sweetcorn kernels (about 3 sweetcorn cobs)
60 ml (¼ cup) evaporated milk
100 g (3½ oz) caster (superfine) sugar
150 g (5½ oz) unsalted butter, softened, plus extra for greasing
5 large eggs, separated
75 g (½ cup) plain (all-purpose) flour, sifted

Preheat the oven to 180°C (350°F). Grease a deep 1.5 litre (51 fl oz) baking dish with butter.

Pulse the corn in a blender with the milk and sugar, until chopped into small chunks (we want to retain some texture inside the cake).

Place the butter in the bowl of a stand mixer with the whisk attached and beat on medium speed until smooth. Add the egg yolks one at a time, beating well between each addition, then add the flour and mix until well combined. Stir in the corn mixture, using a spatula.

Using a different, clean bowl, beat the egg whites on high speed until firm peaks form, then fold the meringue into the cake batter using a spatula in slow movements.

Pour the mixture into the prepared dish, cover with foil and bake for 50 minutes or until a skewer inserted into the centre of the cake comes out clean.

Preheat the grill (broiler) to medium–high. Remove the foil from the baking dish and grill the cake for 5 minutes to create a lovely crispy golden finish.

Allow the cake to cool to room temperature, then cut into slices and serve. The cake will keep in an airtight container in the fridge for up to 1 week.

TAMALES DE CHOCOLATE

CHOCOLATE TAMALES

Sometimes the dishes you miss the most open up new creative pathways. That was the case for me with tamales. When I moved to Australia, I had to learn how to make them – and make them to the point of perfection! I am proud to be called the Tamale Queen because these are now my signature – and favourite – dish at my restaurants. After such an extensive chapter of tamales in my first cookbook, *Comida Mexicana*, I decided just to add this dessert version here (perfect if you ever need a gluten-free dessert). I'm using Mexican chocolate here, but you can use any other chocolate powder mixed with water ... after all, cacao beans are originally from Mexico!

20 sweetcorn husks (see Note)
180 g (6½ oz) Mexican chocolate, shaved
200 g (7 oz) pork lard
2 teaspoons baking powder
400 g (14 oz) caster (superfine) sugar
500 g (1 lb 2 oz) masa flour
200 g (7 oz) chocolate hazelnut spread
  (such as Nutella)

Soften the sweetcorn husks in warm water, then drain and squeeze the husks to remove any excess water.

Place the chocolate in a bowl and add 400 ml (14 fl oz) of warm water. Set aside for 10 minutes, stirring often, until the chocolate dissolves.

Place the lard, baking powder and sugar in a bowl and whip the mixture as fast as possible using a wooden spoon – the lard needs to soften and look spongy. Don't stress if this takes a long time; it can take up to 15 minutes to achieve the right consistency. Add the flour and watery chocolate and mix until well combined.

Spread 100 g (3½ oz) of the dough in the middle of a damp sweetcorn husk, leaving a 3 cm (1¼ in) border around the edge. Spoon 1 tablespoon of the hazelnut spread on top, then cover with another 100 g (3½ oz) of dough. Place another sweetcorn husk over the filling, then wrap up the tamale by overlapping the sides and folding over the top and bottom edges towards the centre to enclose the filling. Secure the ends with kitchen string and set aside. Repeat to make 10 tamales.

Stand the tamales upright in a large steamer, but don't pack them in too tightly or they might burst. Place the steamer over a saucepan of simmering water and steam for 1 hour or until the husks peel away easily. Allow the tamales to cool for 15 minutes, then unwrap and serve.

NOTE

YOU CAN BUY DRIED SWEETCORN HUSKS FROM LATIN AMERICAN SUPERMARKETS OR ONLINE.

ENSALADA DE MANZANA

APPLE SALAD

You will find ensalada de manzana all year round at any mercado and even at weddings, but come Christmas this apple salad is what every chilango in the city expects to see on the dinner table. To you, this might seem more like a dessert, however, it is actually served as a salad, so here we go.

I keep this beautiful Christmas tradition in Sydney – my sister Ana is in charge of making it every year as she is well known for having the sweeter tooth of us.

6 sweet apples, peeled, cored and cut
    into 1.5 cm (½ in) dice
395 g (13½ oz) tin condensed milk
2 tablespoons finely diced pecans
2 tablespoons sultanas (golden raisins)
2½ tablespoons thickened cream
227 g (8 oz) tin pineapple pieces in syrup, drained
    and cut into 1.5 cm (½ in) dice
glace cherries in syrup, drained, to serve

Combine all of the ingredients except the glace cherries in a bowl. Set aside in the fridge for 1 hour for the flavours to develop.

Decorate the salad with a few glace cherries and serve.

ARROZ DE TRES LECHES

RICE PUDDING

There is no other person in my family who makes such delicious rice pudding as my sister Ana. I got the recipe from her not long ago. (I suspect I didn't learn to make it earlier because hers was always there to spoil me!)

This is quite unlike a normal rice pudding made with plain milk – the condensed milk gives it an incredible sweetness. I love my sister and I envy her sweet tooth! She can just keep eating desserts, cakes, sweets and anything else she craves!

395 g (13½ oz) tin condensed milk
340 ml (11½ fl oz) tin evaporated milk
250 ml (1 cup) full-cream (whole) milk
2 cinnamon sticks
1 tablespoon vanilla essence
200 g (1 cup) jasmine rice, rinsed
1½ tablespoons sultanas (golden raisins; optional)
1 teaspoon ground cinnamon

Place the three milks, cinnamon sticks and vanilla essence in a heavy-based saucepan over low heat. Bring just to the boil, stirring constantly, then remove from the heat and set aside for the cinnamon to infuse.

Add the rice and 750 ml (3 cups) of water to a separate saucepan and set over medium–low heat. Bring to the boil and cook for 10 minutes or until the rice is just beginning to soften. Add the milk mixture and cook, stirring occasionally, for 30 minutes or until the rice is tender and the mixture is quite thick. Stir through the sultanas (if using).

Enjoy the arroz de tres leches warm or cold, with the ground cinnamon dusted over the top.

BORRACHITOS

'LITTLE DRUNKS'

The peculiar name 'borrachitos' means 'little drunks', and it points its finger at one of the most important ingredients in this recipe: rum. These small rectangular sweets are originally from Puebla. There are a few manufactured brands, but it's more common to find these sold fresh from large baskets outside mercados that offer traditional desserts. You can find them in different colours but the original version is red, so I'm using red jelly here.

115 g (½ cup) caster (superfine) sugar, plus extra for rolling
120 g (4 oz) red jelly (jello) crystals
50 g (⅓ cup) cornflour (cornstarch)
60 ml (¼ cup) white rum (you can also use tequila)

Bring 250 ml (1 cup) of water to the boil over medium heat, then reduce the heat to low, add the sugar and stir to combine. Add the red jelly crystals and stir until the sugar and crystals are completely dissolved.

In a bowl, combine the cornflour and 50 ml (1¾ fl oz) of water, then add it to the jelly mixture. Stir constantly for 3–4 minutes, until the mixture is thick and starting to boil. Remove from the heat and allow to cool for 10 minutes, then stir through the rum. Spoon the mixture into a 20 cm x 14 cm (8 in x 5½ in) tin or glass dish, then transfer to the fridge for at least 3 hours, until firm.

Cut the borrachito into 5 cm x 3 cm (2 in x 1¼ in) rectangular jellies and roll them in extra sugar to coat.

Keep the borrachitos in an airtight container in the fridge for up to 1 week.

SALSAS SALSAS

A MEAL WITHOUT

'Comida sin chile no es comida.'

CHILLI IS NOT A MEAL.

Corn and chilli are the oldest ingredients in the kitchens of Mexico. We have coloured corn to make funky tortillas, and we might even fight among ourselves over which is the best. But there is something that would always reunite us, and that is chillies! All the varieties, all the species and, together with more ingredients, made into salsas! It is this simple word that unifies our country. It doesn't matter where in Mexico you are, salsas will always be part of the meal.

There are factory-produced salsas, such as Valentina, Botanera, Meridana, Buffalo or San Luis, and those that are freshly made at home – green, red, tatemada, borracha, macha and others – either blended with a molcajete (mortar and pestle) or an electric blender. Mexicans enjoy every single one of them and we are lucky enough to have thousands to choose from, in part because they are made with our huge range of chillies.

My favourite memory of trying salsas in Mexico City is when I went with my friend Gil to eat tacos. Everyone knew how good this particular taco stall was and we made the long journey all the way out there. I ordered my tacos 'con todo' (with the lot), even though I wasn't good with chilli then. Well, it didn't end up as much fun as I expected. The salsas were amazingly tasty, but very, very spicy! I cried all the way back home, drinking mango juice and regretting my decision of going 'with the lot'. Please remember to order tacos 'sin salsa' and try before you add your own sauce, rather than letting the taquero add it for you. Salsas in Mexico City are free, so you can always help yourself once you've tasted your taco. And then you can try the different options – they usually have two or three available.

Feel free to add any of these salsas to any dish, even non-Mexican ones!

PICO DE GALLO

FRESH SALSA

S E R V E S 4

S E R V E S 4

I love that pico de gallo is becoming more popular outside of Mexico. It's an easy, healthy and versatile salsa that can be used as a salad, side, topping or filling. I highly recommend you try it with different dishes to find your favourite pairing – I especially love to serve pico de gallo with roast chicken tacos … it's the best!

½ white onion, diced
4 green jalapeno, serrano or Thai chillies,
  finely chopped
handful of coriander (cilantro) leaves,
  finely chopped
juice of 2 limes
1 teaspoon table salt
3 tomatoes, diced into 3 cm (1¼ in) cubes

Place the onion, chilli and coriander in a bowl, add the lime juice and salt and gently stir for 3 minutes. Add the tomato, stir and serve straight away.

Pico de gallo is best eaten on the day it is made.

SERVES 4

SALSA VERDE DE CHILE ASADO

ROASTED GREEN SALSA

Salsa verde comes in myriad versions and can be mixed with a huge range of ingredients, the most common being tomatillos and jalapenos. In Mexico City it is easy to find salsa verde made only with a mix of chillies. This version is called roasted salsa, and I love it for tacos dorados. Many street vendors selling tacos de canasta and tacos de carnitas will offer this salsa. The vibrant colour and spicy smell of the chillies is what makes you respect it!

10 green serrano chillies, stems removed
5 fresh jalapeno chillies, stems removed
½ white onion, roughly chopped
1 garlic clove, peeled
1 teaspoon table salt
oil cooking spray

Place the chillies, onion, garlic and salt in a saucepan over medium heat, spray with oil and cook, covered and stirring occasionally, for about 7 minutes, until charred.

Transfer the ingredients to a molcajete or a blender, add 250 ml (1 cup) of water and pound or blend until smooth – the mixture should be quite thick.

Store in an airtight container in the fridge for up to 1 week.

MOLCAJETE!
MOLCAJETE!
MOLCAJETE!
MOLCAJETE!
MOLCAJETE!
MOLCAJETE!
MOLCAJETE!

(MEXICO'S TRADITIONAL MORTAR AND PESTLE)

MEXICAN MOLCAJETES ARE BEAUTIFULLY HAND-SHAPED STANDING BOWLS MADE OF VOLCANIC STONE.

Although they might look like unwieldy pre-Hispanic utensils, molcajetes are still present in Mexican kitchens. Especially in country towns, where there are families still dedicated to hand-crafting them. In places where life moves not as fast as in the city, local cooks use molcajetes to blend ingredients for salsas, moles, powders, guacamoles and more.

Angelita, my abuelita on my mother's side, was from a very small town in the state of Puebla. She was very familiar with molcajetes, metates (grinding stones) and all sorts of traditional Mexican utensils – partly because her town didn't have electricity until recent years. When she came to visit us in the city, she would bring rare ingredients from her farm to cook for us. She always used the molcajete instead of the electric blender; I never understood her obsession with it, as the dishes seemed to take longer than if she'd used modern techniques! It wasn't until years later that I came to understand the importance of keeping our traditions alive. My palate grew into the ability to taste the different flavours of something made in a molcajete.

Molcajetes are easy enough to find outside of Mexico – I have them available at my own shops. I highly recommend buying a volcanic stone molcajete, instead of the volcanic sand, marble or ceramic varieties, as it will give additional flavour to your food. A good molcajete should be porous, slightly crooked because of their hand-made nature, and have three small triangular legs. The bowl always comes with a tejolote – a thick triangular stone pestle – and a hand-made escobetilla made of natural zacaton fibres tied together to make a cleaning brush. You need to cure your molcajete before it can begin its cooking journey:

1. Place it upside down with the tejolote in a bucket of clean warm water. Leave it to soak for 2 hours so it fully hydrates, then drain.

2. Add 80 g (2¾ oz) of uncooked beans to the molcajete and crush with the tejolote, polishing the stone with strong but slow circular movements. Avoid hitting the molcajete. Brush off as much powder as you can – don't worry too much.

3. Repeat with 50 g (1¾ oz) of rice and 20 g (¾ oz) of cooking salt together in the molcajete. Brush off.

4. Rinse the molcajete under cold water until the water runs clear – it can sometimes take up to six polishes with rice and salt for the molcajete to be ready.

GUACAMOLE FALSO

FAKE GUACAMOLE

Guacamole is one of Mexico's favourite salsas. However, the large amount of avocados used every day per stall, and their increasing price, affects businesses and so we turn to other recipes such as our famous 'secret guacamole'.

I discovered this secret not long ago and it was exciting for our Mexican community in Australia – we all recognised the flavour and consistency and it bought back memories of our favourite taco stalls. Have it on your table for topping tacos or quesadillas or just to scoop up with some totopos.

If you can't find tomatillos, you can use green capsicum here.

5 fresh or tinned tomatillos
2 Lebanese or green zucchini (courgette), chopped
5 green jalapeno or serrano chillies, stems removed, roughly chopped
½ white onion, chopped
small handful of coriander (cilantro) leaves, including a few stems
2 teaspoons table salt
juice of 1 lime
1 tablespoon vegetable oil
1 teaspoon white vinegar

If you are lucky enough to find fresh tomatillos, remove the husks and thoroughly wash the fruit. If using tinned tomatillos, drain and rinse them. Roughly chop the tomatillos.

Blend all the ingredients together to reach a creamy consistency. Do not add water as it'll ruin the secret!

Store in an airtight container in the fridge for up to 5 days.

GUACAMOLE

I make my guacamole using a mortar and pestle. It has a better flavour and I even like to present it that way on the table. If you are lucky enough to be at a weekday street market in Mexico, find yourself the guacamole stall. You'll be delighted and amazed by the size of the mortar and pestle, the flavour and colour of the guacamole and, of course, the price!

I have seen guacamole topped with pepitas, pomegranate seeds, sliced habanero, red onion, lime zest, chicatana ants and even crickets. But the most common topping in Mexico City is diced tomato – it gives contrast and colour and the combination is just perfect. And wherever guacamole is served, totopos or chicharrones are usually nearby!

1 small garlic clove
5 small avocados, halved
1 tomato, seeds removed, diced
3 teaspoons table salt
2 green jalapeno, serrano or Thai chillies, chopped
1 tablespoon olive oil
large handful of coriander (cilantro), chopped
juice of 3 limes

Gently pound the garlic clove in a mortar and pestle, then add the avocado and mash to a chunky paste. Add the remaining ingredients and stir to combine until you have a thick and luscious guacamole.

Guacamole is best eaten on the day it is made, as the avocado will start to discolour once peeled. If you have leftovers, check out the fake guacamole opposite and mix them together, then add to different dishes or use as a salsa to top your tacos.

GUACAMOLE
FALSO
PAGE 212

GUACAMOLE
PAGE 213

SALSA DE CACAHUATE Y CHILE DE ÁRBOL

PEANUT & CHILE DE ÁRBOL SALSA

I remember eating this salsa whenever my grandma came to visit. My dear abuelita came from a small village in Puebla called Agua Fria. This picturesque little hamlet is where my mum grew up and I love the fact that trading still takes place among the small community. They grow and produce bread, salsas, milk, cheeses, corn and much more. Saying this, my abuelita would always bring different ingredients, flavours and dishes with her and, of course, her magic touch to everything she cooked – including this super-spicy salsa.

I'd spread it lightly on a sandwich, quesadilla or steak – always being careful because, remember, the salsa is as spicy as the person who made it. And Mexican abuelitas are dangerous!

I usually make this salsa with chile de árbol, as the chilli Abuelita used is not easy to find outside of Mexico. But if you are lucky enough to find chiltepin chilli, buy some, as that's the one for this salsa!

125 ml (½ cup) olive oil
4 garlic cloves
20 dried chiles de árbol
50 g (1¾ oz) unsalted raw peanuts
1 teaspoon table salt
pinch of black pepper

Heat 60 ml (¼ cup) of the oil in a saucepan over medium heat, add the garlic and fry, stirring, until browned on both sides (not burnt). Using a slotted spoon, scoop the garlic into a molcajete or blender, then add the chillies to the oil, reduce the heat to low and cook, stirring, for 3 minutes until dark red in colour (no more than that or they'll taste bitter). Transfer the chillies to the molcajete or blender.

Add the remaining oil and the peanuts to the pan and fry, stirring constantly, for 6 minutes or until lightly browned. Add the peanuts to the garlic and chillies and set the oil aside to cool to room temperature.

Add 125 ml (½ cup) of water to the molcajete or blender, along with the salt and pepper, and pound or blend until smooth. Transfer the salsa to a serving bowl and stir through the cooled oil until completely incorporated.

Store any leftover salsa in an airtight container in the pantry for up to 6 months.

MAKES ABOUT 500 G (2 CUPS)

SALSA DE SIETE CHILES

SEVEN CHILLI SALSA

If seven sounds like a lot of chillies and you're worried you might not enjoy this, well, take a chance! I dare you to try it – and I guarantee you will fall in love with it, just like I did! If you feel it's going to be too super-spicy for you, the first time you make it just add more tomatoes to dilute it down.

125 ml (½ cup) vegetable oil
1 dried pasilla chilli
3 dried morita chillies
2 dried chipotle chillies
3 dried cascabel chillies
2 dried guajillo chillies
3 dried chiles de árbol
1 dried ancho chilli
2 roma (plum) tomatoes, quartered
6 garlic cloves, peeled
125 ml (½ cup) white vinegar
1 tablespoon dried epazote
2½ teaspoons table salt

Heat 60 ml (¼ cup) of the oil in a saucepan over medium heat. Add all the chillies and cook, stirring constantly, for about 3 minutes or until they have an oily sheen. Remove the chillies using a slotted spoon and drain on paper towel, then set aside to cool. Remove the stems.

Add the tomato and garlic to the pan and cook, stirring frequently, for 5 minutes or until the garlic is lightly browned. Transfer to a blender and allow to cool. Leave the oil in the pan to cool to room temperature.

Add the remaining oil and the cooled oil in the pan to the blender, along with the chillies, vinegar, epazote and salt. Blend to a shiny, slightly dense salsa.

Store the salsa in an airtight container in the fridge for up to 1 week.

SALSA DE
ZANAHORIA
CON HABANERO

PAGE 220

SALSA DE
SIETE CHILES

PAGE 217

SALSA DE CACAHUATE Y CHILE DE ÁRBOL
PAGE 216

SALSA DE HABANERO CON MANGO
PAGE 221

SALSA DE ZANAHORIA CON HABANERO

CARROT SALSA WITH HABANERO

The simplicity of this salsa recipe belies its flavour, colour and versatility. Although it's not commonly served in the city, it's one of the favourites at La Cocina de Chayito, a humble stall where Chayo the owner cooks up a huge menu. You'd better be hungry when you go there, as she'll try to feed you a lot! Her salsas are always a delight and her creativity is to use whatever is leftover or on hand. So, next time you have a couple of carrots waiting in your fridge, just bring them out and transform them into Chayo's amazing salsa!

2 habanero chillies (preferably orange, yellow or red)
2 carrots (about 350 g/12½ oz), roughly chopped
½ white onion
1 garlic clove
1 teaspoon table salt

Char the habanero chillies in a dry comal or heavy-based frying pan over medium heat for 5 minutes, stirring constantly, until they begin to soften and blacken. Remove the chillies from the pan and carefully remove the stems, then transfer to a blender, along with the carrot, onion, garlic, salt and 50 ml (1¾ fl oz) of water. Blend to create a chunky salsa, then transfer to a serving bowl.

The salsa goes really well with tostadas, flautas, tacos dorados, pambazos or any other creamy dish.

Store leftovers in an airtight container in the fridge for up to 1 week.

SALSA DE HABANERO CON MANGO

HABANERO SALSA WITH MANGO

Habanero, being a fruity chilli, always pairs well with mango. I saw this salsa a lot on my last trip to Mexico. I liked this version in particular, as it is made with fresh ingredients and you get the chance to add more mango when you taste it, to make it more sweet and less spicy. Blended, this salsa is perfect for dipping totopos or chicken wings. Alternatively, you can mix it so some of the ingredients are blended and others chopped, so it feels fresh and chunky.

   This salsa is great with tacos de cochinita pibil or seafood, and you can also make it with papaya or cucumber instead of mango.

2–3 habanero chillies
60 ml (¼ cup) orange juice
juice of 2 lemons
1 mango (about 200 g/7 oz), finely chopped
1 red onion, finely diced
2 teaspoons table salt
pinch of black pepper

Char the habanero chillies in a dry comal or heavy-based frying pan over medium heat for 7–10 minutes, stirring constantly, until they begin to soften and blacken slightly. Remove the chillies from the pan and carefully remove the stems, then transfer to a blender, along with the orange and lemon juice, mango, onion, salt, pepper and 50 ml (1¾ fl oz) of water, and blend until smooth.

Store any leftovers in an airtight container in the fridge for up to 1 week.

SALSA CHAMOY

CHAMOY SALSA

S E R V E S 8

S E R V E S 8

There is no doubt that chamoy has positioned itself as one of the star sauces of Mexico City. It is eaten with snacks, mocktails, cocktails, beer, candy, gummy bears, seafood, fruits, vegetables and even by itself. There are some commercial brands that are easily found at Latin American grocers; however, making it at home gives you control over the flavours and freedom to add different fruits and play with the consistency. Spicy, salty, citrusy, sweet, tangy, acid, sour ... all at once! I love chamoy, especially in micheladas.

150 g (1 cup) dried apricots, roughly chopped
2 tablespoons tamarind puree
20 g (¾ oz) chopped dried plums (see Note)
20 g (¾ oz) dried hibiscus flowers (see Note)
1 dried guajillo chilli, stem and seeds removed
110 g (½ cup) brown sugar
2 teaspoons Tajin seasoning
1 tablespoon Mexican chilli powder
juice of 2 limes
juice of 1 orange

Place the apricot, tamarind, plum, hibiscus, chilli and 250 ml (1 cup) of water in a saucepan, bring to the boil, then reduce the heat to medium and simmer, stirring occasionally, for 30 minutes or until the mixture is dark red in colour. Add the sugar, Tajin and chilli powder and continue to cook, stirring, until the sugar is dissolved. Remove from the heat and set aside to cool for 30 minutes.

Depending on how you're going to enjoy the chamoy, you can blend it to a smooth consistency, strain it into a jar or leave it chunky – it's your choice! Whichever you choose, add the lime juice and orange juice and stir until incorporated.

Chamoy is so much fun to eat, it'll make all your taste buds have a party! Want to go a bit crazy? Try adding mango, pineapple, green apple, blueberries or even strawberries!

Store the chamoy in an airtight container or jar in the fridge for up to 6 months.

Chamoy variations

◆ Blend to a thick consistency that's perfect for a sticky michelada rim.

◆ Stir through 125 ml (½ cup) of water to make a pourable chamoy that's perfect for serving over fruits and vegetables.

◆ Add a further 125 ml (½ cup) of lime juice and serve alongside freshly cooked seafood for dipping.

NOTE

DRIED PLUMS CAN BE PURCHASED FROM ASIAN SUPERMARKETS. LOOK FOR DRIED HIBISCUS FLOWERS AT YOUR LOCAL LATIN AMERICAN OR AFRICAN GROCER.

FRIJOLES NEGROS

BLACK BEANS

What kind of Mexican cookbook would this be without a recipe for black beans? I remember helping my grandma clean frijoles when we would buy them in Mexico City. I enjoyed the time spent with her, plus I'd get excited if I found any foreign items, like grit or stones. We once had a pressure cooker accident, when the lid flew off and there were beans everywhere in the kitchen – even on the ceiling – which made me scared of the pressure cooker for a long time! But using a pressure cooker to cook beans will save you time.

I like to have beans on hand always, as they can be added to any dish as a side and they are good to bulk up your meals, so I cook mine in big batches. You need to start this recipe the day before.

250 g (9 oz) dried black beans
½ white onion
1 bay leaf
pinch of epazote (optional)
3 teaspoons table salt

Rinse the beans and remove any grit or small rocks, then place in a large bowl and cover with water. Set aside to soak overnight.

The next day, drain and rinse the beans, then place in a large saucepan with the onion, bay leaf, epazote (if using) and 1.5 litres (51 fl oz) of water. Bring to the boil over high heat and boil the beans for 30 minutes, then reduce the heat to medium and simmer for a further 40 minutes or until the beans are soft and cooked through. If the pan starts to dry out, add up to 250 ml (1 cup) more water. Drain the beans, reserving the cooking water – you may need it for other recipes. Remove and discard the bay leaf and onion, then add the salt and stir.

Transfer the frijoles to a bowl and serve or add to your dish of choice. Any leftovers will keep in an airtight container in the fridge for up to 5 days.

FRIJOLES REFRITOS

REFRIED BLACK BEANS

There are many opportunities to buy refried beans in Mexico City – you can find them tinned, bagged and even dehydrated. This is one of the basic dishes that can be used to accompany pretty much anything, and you can make this recipe using pinto, red or gueros (white) beans, too.

Refried beans are simple to make and incredibly versatile. Try adding chorizo, crumbled Cotija, panela, queso fresco or feta, or slices of jalapeno or habanero chilli.

2 tablespoons vegetable oil
½ white or brown onion, finely chopped
3 tomatoes, finely diced
1 x quantity Frijoles negros, plus 125 ml (½ cup) reserved bean cooking water (see opposite)
pinch of epazote (optional)

Heat the oil in a large frying pan over medium heat, add the onion and tomato and cook, stirring occasionally, for about 8 minutes, until the tomato starts to collapse and the onion is soft.

Add the frijoles and reserved cooking water and, using a potato masher, crush the beans until they are half mashed, adding a little extra water if the mixture is very thick.

Add the epazote (if using) and stir the beans for 3 minutes or until heated through.

Transfer the refried beans to a bowl and serve or add to your dish of choice. Any leftovers will keep in an airtight container in the fridge for up to 5 days.

TORTILLAS DE MAIZ
CORN TORTILLAS

What's the difference between nixtamal and cornmeal tortillas? Nixtamal is a Nahuatl word that means 'masa' and 'ash' – the process involves cooking corn kernels with limewater, then grinding them to make dough (masa), which is then pressed into tortillas using a machine or tortilla press. It is the traditional and best way to make tortillas, but it's also a time- and labour-intensive process.

In this recipe we are going to use cornmeal, as it is easier to find. Cornmeal is made from cooked corn – brands like Maseca and Minsa are the most popular and I have found them at Latin American markets, even in Europe. Some Asian or Indian supermarkets also sell cornmeal, but labelled as 'maize flour'. I keep maize flour at home always, as it saves me from emergencies that Mexicans dread, like there not being any tortillas at the supermarket!

500 g (1 lb 2 oz) masa flour (yellow, white or blue)
pinch of salt
50 ml (1¾ fl oz) vegetable oil
oil cooking spray

Combine the masa, 600 ml (20½ fl oz) of warm water, the salt and oil in a bowl until you have a soft and non-sticky dough.

Lightly spray a comal or heavy-based frying pan with oil spray and place over medium–high heat. Place a square of plastic wrap over the bottom half of a tortilla press. Roll 50 g (1¾ oz) of the dough into a ball and place it in the middle of the press. Cover with another square of plastic wrap, then close the press and gently push down to flatten the dough into a 16 cm (6¼ in) tortilla, about 3 mm (⅛ mm) thick.

Open the tortilla press, remove the top layer of plastic wrap and flip the tortilla onto your hand. Remove the bottom layer of plastic wrap and place the tortilla in the comal or pan. Cook for about 2 minutes each side or until the tortilla puffs up and the edge is just starting to change colour. Transfer the cooked tortilla to a tortilla warmer or wrap in a folded tea towel, then repeat with the remaining dough.

Leftover tortillas will keep in a tortilla warmer in the fridge for up to 4 days. Gently reheat in a comal or microwave (wrap eight tortillas in a tea towel and cook on High for 1 minute), or use them to make tostadas (see page 233) or Totopos (see page 232).

TORTILLAS DE HARINA

FLOUR TORTILLAS

Tortillas de harina are very well known throughout the world, but many people think they are from the USA rather than Mexico. Well, I am here to confirm that they are indeed a popular Mexican ingredient that originates from the state of Sonora in the north of the country. Flour tortillas taste way better when freshly made, ready to wrap up into a burrito, sandwiched together to make quesadillas and sincronizadas, or even deep-fried to make bunuelos (doughnut fritters).

There used to be a flour tortilla shop in my local mercado in Claveria; my dad used to take us there early on Saturday mornings to grab a bunch of tortillas to eat with cajeta (thick caramel). You see, unlike corn tortillas, tortillas de harina go well with both savoury and sweet fillings, making them very versatile. Here is one of my best-kept secrets that shouldn't be shared: I prefer flour tortillas to corn tortillas ... shhhhh!

500 g (3⅓ cups) plain (all-purpose) flour, plus extra for dusting
80 g (⅓ cup) vegetable shortening or lard
2 pinches of table salt
1 teaspoon baking powder
220 ml (8 fl oz) warm water (as hot as your hands can handle)

Place the flour, vegetable shortening or lard, salt, baking powder and half the water in a bowl and mix together using your hands to form a rough dough. Add more water as needed and knead until you have a soft and elastic dough – this will take about 15 minutes. Completely cover the dough with a wet clean tea towel and set aside to rest for 20 minutes.

On a work surface lightly dusted with flour, roll the dough into 40 g (1½ oz) balls, then use a rolling pin to roll them out to 14 cm (5½ in) tortillas.

Heat a comal or heavy-based frying pan over medium heat. Add 1–2 tortillas and cook for about 20 seconds, then flip and cook the other side until the tortillas have a few brownish dots. Flip again and let the tortillas inflate like a balloon, then remove and place in a tortilla warmer or folded clean tea towel. Repeat with the remaining dough.

Store leftover tortillas in an airtight container in the fridge for up to 5 days. To reheat, heat a comal or heavy-based frying pan over medium heat and cook the tortillas for about 2 minutes, flipping until warmed through. Alternatively, wrap up to eight tortillas in a tea towel and microwave on High for about 1 minute.

TOTOPOS

TORTILLA CHIPS

The large variety of totopos in Australia is amazing, from classic to beetroot, spinach, jalapeno and even nopal (prickly pear) flavours. This traditional Mexican snack is conquering supermarkets and even in-flight snacks! I was surprised to be served mini round totopos with salsa on a plane trip to Tasmania where I was taking part in a festival dedicated to empowering young women. I was to give a talk about Mexican gastronomy and teach some of the basics. The girls were very much engaged, and had so much fun learning how to make tortillas and then grill them and cut into shapes for frying or baking into crispy, golden, salty totopos. I truly hope I planted a seed of Mexican food in their hearts!

500 ml (2 cups) vegetable oil
15 Tortillas de maiz (see page 228)
table salt, to taste

Heat the oil in a large heavy-based saucepan over medium–high heat to 180°C (350°F) on a kitchen thermometer.

Cut the tortillas into triangles and, working in batches so as not to overcrowd the pan, add the tortilla triangles to the hot oil and fry, flipping frequently, for 3 minutes or until crisp and lightly golden.

Remove the tortillas using a slotted spoon and transfer to a large plate lined with paper towel to drain. Season with salt and serve with your favourite sides.

TOSTADAS

Tostadas are the Mexican version of toasties. They are used in many dishes or as a base for thousands of toppings – I remember eating them just with cream and salsa when I lived in the city.

A tostada is simply a deep-fried corn tortilla. You can also dry-toast the tortillas in a comal over low heat until crisp, but watch carefully that they don't burn.

You will find a few dishes in this cookbook that specify to serve with tostadas, but feel free to add them anywhere you like – either by themselves or topped with a nice thick cream, avocado, cheese, refried beans, salsa ….

vegetable oil, for shallow-frying
10 Tortillas de maiz (see page 228)

Heat 100 ml (3½ fl oz) of vegetable oil in a large frying pan over medium heat to 180°C (350°F) on a kitchen thermometer. Fry the tortillas, one by one, flipping frequently and adding 50 ml (1¾ fl oz) of extra oil after every three tostadas, for about 2 minutes, until they are crisp and lightly golden. If bubbles start to rise in the tortillas when they are cooking, use tongs to pinch the holes together. Transfer the tostadas to a plate lined with paper towel to drain.

If you prefer, you can dry-toast the tortillas in a comal over low heat, flipping frequently, until crisp.

TOTOPOS
PAGE 232

TOSTADAS
PAGE 233

ARROZ MEXICANO

MEXICAN RICE

I have such memories of the marvellous smell from all the kitchens around Mexico City as they prepared rice 'Mexican-style' to be part of the daily comida corrida. Every day this rice would be cooked – especially at lunchtime – to fill up workers with a large, good-value meal at the fondas and cocinas economicas of every suburb.

250 g (9 oz) long-grain rice
2 large (about 250 g/9 oz) roma (plum) tomatoes, roughly chopped
½ small white onion, roughly chopped
90 g (⅓ cup) tomato paste (concentrated puree)
1 teaspoon table salt
400 ml (14 fl oz) chicken stock or water
1 tablespoon vegetable oil
2 garlic cloves, peeled
2 Thai green chillies

Soak the rice in a bowl of cold water for 10 minutes. Drain and rinse.

Place the tomato, onion, tomato paste, salt and chicken stock or water in a blender and blend until smooth – you need 500 ml (2 cups) of liquid for this recipe.

Heat the oil in a large saucepan over medium–low heat. Add the garlic and cook, stirring, for 1–2 minutes, until lightly browned. Using a slotted spoon, remove the garlic cloves and discard. Add the drained rice to the pan and stir for 8 minutes or until lightly toasted. Add the blended tomato mixture and stir to combine, then cover and cook for 15 minutes.

Score 5 mm (¼ in) long slits all over the chillies, then add them to the pan. Gently stir the rice, then cover and continue to cook, adding more water if the mixture starts to look dry, for a further 3 minutes or until the liquid has evaporated and the rice is cooked through.

Transfer the rice to serving bowls and serve.

JALAPENOS TOREADOS

BLISTERED JALAPENOS

I love being able to buy fresh jalapenos in Australia. Every time I visit the supermarket I always end up buying at least a couple to spice up my meals or, in this case, to grill and keep in a big jar for whenever I have a craving.

I remember, when I was living in Mexico City, making tacos de carne asada with my friends. We would share the cooking tasks and I was usually in charge of pouring all the sauces into the jalapeno jar. The fun of this is that you can add more or less of any ingredient – your choice!

10 fresh jalapeno chillies
1 teaspoon garlic salt
1 tablespoon Valentina hot sauce
1 teaspoon Maggi seasoning
1 teaspoon Worcestershire sauce
juice of 1 lime

Char the jalapeno chillies in a dry comal or heavy-based frying pan over medium heat for 15 minutes, stirring frequently, until they blacken.

Place the chillies in a clean 1 litre (34 fl oz) jar and add the garlic salt, Valentina sauce, Maggi seasoning, Worcestershire sauce and lime juice. Screw on the lid securely and shake the jar to combine the ingredients.

Enjoy straight away or store in the fridge for up to 1 week.

NOTE

I LOVE MAKING BIG BATCHES OF THESE JALAPENOS SO I ALWAYS HAVE SOMETHING SPICY ON HAND TO ADD TO MY MEALS; YOU CAN ALSO ADD SAUTEED SLICED ONION.

FOOD LOVERS' GUIDE

IF YOU WANT TO EXPERIENCE THE FOOD OF MEXICO CITY 'CHILANGO' STYLE, HERE IS MY GUIDE TO THE BEST CAFES, RESTAURANTS, MARKETS AND BARS THAT I ALWAYS VISIT WHEN I'M IN CDMX (AND THAT TOURISTS DON'T KNOW ABOUT!).

TACOS

1

CARNICERIA LA MEJOR

IRAPUATO 51, CLAVERIA, AZCAPOTZALCO

This is a very popular spot in front of El Mercado de Claveria; you can't miss it as it's always packed with a huge queue, especially on Thursdays when the street market is open. La Mejor's deep-fried pork carnitas tacos are some of the best in the city and their aroma fills the neighbourhood from morning to mid-afternoon (also try their deep-fried-in-lard gorditas, which are crunchilicious!). Salsa roja with big chunks of coriander and onion makes the perfect topping!

Desayunos

1
CAFÉ LA BLANCA

AV. 5 DE MAYO 40,

CENTRO HISTÓRICO

You will find every breakfast option on offer here. They have been trading since 1915 and make their own bread. It is one of my grandpa's favourite spots.

2
NICOS RESTAURANT

AV. CUITLÁHUAC 3102,

CLAVERIA, AZCAPOTZALCO

Their menu is fully Mexican, keeping the traditional recipes with a family atmosphere. Every time I have friends from overseas, I take them to Nicos and they all love it. The salsas are great and the 'café con leche' is a must!

3
LONCHERIA LA RAMBLA

CALLE DE MOTOLINIA 38,

CENTRO HISTÓRICO

One of the oldest sincronizada places. Try the chillies in vinegar, the guacamole and the crispy tortillas. Afterwards, spend the day wandering around Centro Histórico – there are a million things to do and you might be lucky enough to enjoy a free dancing lesson or some live music.

4
EL BORREGO VIUDO

AV. REVOLUCIÓN 241, TACUBAYA,

MIGUEL HIDALGO

This is one of the most popular barbaboca places in the city and the main attraction is that they are open 24/7 the whole year. Their lamb stock will instantly cure any morning hangover, so make sure you head there after a big night out.

2
EL TURIX LEGARIA

CALZ LEGARIA 449, PANTEÓN FRANCÉS,

MIGUEL HIDALGO

This is my favourite place for cochinita pibil – and it's the only dish you'll find here! This small street-food stall sits outside the cemetery where my relatives rest, alongside famous singers, painters and artists. A tostada de cochinita pibil is always comforting after a visit, but make sure you order the tacos as well with their habanero and onion sauce!

3
LOS ESPECIALES

AVENIDA FRANCISCO I. MADERO 71

CENTRO HISTÓRICO

There is no shortage of places to enjoy tacos in the centre of the city, but if you are after a light bite, the canasta tacos at Los Especiales cannot be missed. This is the number one spot for canasta tacos in the city – the chicharrón is my favourite, and the salsa verde is compulsory!

4
COSTILLAS AL CARBÓN 'EL PAISA'

CALLE CLAVELINAS 124, NUEVA SANTA MARIA,

AZCAPOTZALCO

In addition to excellent tacos, Costillas Al Carbón specialise in charcoal ribs, alambres and huge gringas, all served with their special salsas. The famous ice cream shop, La Michoacana, is next door and will provide the perfect agua fresca to match your meal.

Sopas

1

LA POLAR

CALLE GUILLERMO PRIETO 129,

SAN RAFAEL, CUAUHTÉMOC

La Polar is a family cantina that serves one of the best birrias in the city. It has been trading for more than 80 years with the same quality and fun atmosphere, complemented by musicians playing every Mexican favourite mariachi or norteno tunes among the tables. Don't be afraid of ordering a dark beer from the tap, they are the best!

2

CAFÉ DE TACUBA

CALLE DE TACUBA 28,

CENTRO HISTÓRICO

Try the fideo seco at this breathtaking restaurant – one of the oldest in the city and famous for its interior decoration. They always have live music and all meals are prepared as you order, so don't be in a hurry. Every second spent here is worth it.

PETROLERAS

(Big bites)

1

LAS PETROLERAS DE LA GÜERA

CEDROS 75, SAN ANDRES,

AZCAPOTZALCO

La Güera has been running her business for 40 years. Every day she prepares petroleras, hand-made to order with fresh nixtamal yellow masa, pan-fried and topped with different fillings, salsas and cheese. I can never finish one by myself, so I usually go with my son, my little helper! Make sure you are super hungry before heading there as the portions are seriously, ridiculously huge!

2

TORTAS Y TACOS FERRERIA

CERRADA DE LA GRANJAS,

COLONIA EL JAGÜEY

Tortas y Tacos Ferreria is my first food stop whenever I go back to Mexico. They make my favourite tortas! They have a huge range of ingredients for you to create your own torta – but take a look at their suggested combinations, cleverly named after singers or actresses.

3

LA COCINA DE CHAYITO

MERCADO BUGAMBILIA LOCAL 193,

SANTA MARÍA LA RIBERA

You'd better be hungry because the incredible woman who runs La Cocina will try to feed you a lot! She makes one of the best pancitas in the area, as well as chilaquiles, pozole, eggs any style, sopes, flautas, tostadas, comidas corridas, coffee, sweet breads and other unimaginably delicious dishes all from her tiny stall.

3

PIZZA DEL PERRO NEGRO

DONCELES 64,

CENTRO HISTÓRICO

You'll find these pizza restaurants dotted throughout CDMX. The food is extravagant, abundant and as crazy as possible, using Mexican dishes as pizza toppings. Try the chile rellenos pizza: it is to die for!

MARISCOS

1

RESTAURANTE CANTO DE SIRENAS

ATZAYACATL 89, TLAXPANA,

MIGUEL HIDALGO

This once humble little restaurant in the heart of Tlaxpana is now a local seafood institution that has grown to fill almost the whole block, with live music and family entertainment shows, yet still with impeccable food. After filling up on amazing seafood, step outside to see the ladies with huge baskets serving traditional Mexican desserts – don't forget to try them on your way out!

2

LOS JAROCHOS

C. CAMINO A NEXTENGO 188,

SANTA LUCIA, AZCAPOTZALCO

I used to visit Los Jarochos at my local mercado at least once a month for my caldo de camaron hangover cure or whenever I had a random seafood craving. The mercado can get pretty crowded, so I recommend visiting their sister restaurant a few streets away, which sells an equally special caldo de camaron, as well as other seafood favourites including ceviche.

3

TOSTADAS COYOACÁN

MERCADO COYOACÁN, IGNACIO ALLENDE 49,

DEL CARMEN, COYOACÁN

Located inside the Coyoacán Market, Tostadas Coyoacán has a mind-blowing array of tostada fillings on display for you to choose from and mix and match. I highly recommend their seafood tostadas, topped with any of the salsas they have available that are just the perfect combination of flavours. Afterwards, explore this cool suburb with its theatre and crafts market, as well as Frida Carló's home-turned-museum.

DULCES

1

LA ESPECIAL DE PARIS

INSURGENTES CENTRO 117-B,

SAN RAFAEL, CUAUHTÉMOC

This ice-creamery has been trading for more than 100 years. It is where my grandparents used to come when dating, and since then it has been our family ice-creamery of choice. Along with delicious desserts, their amazing ice creams are served with fresh seasonal fruits and unusual ingredients. My favourite is called 'Arlequín' – your choice of five ice-cream flavours, topped with whipped cream, Marie biscuits and crushed pecans!

2

MERCADO DE AMPUDIA

CIRCUNVALACIÓN S/N,

LA MERCED, CENTRO

Traditions, culture and variety collide at this huge 'market of sweets'. Wander through this mercado and you will find all the sweet treats you could possibly imagine. Watch out for bees – they're everywhere!

3

DULCERÍA DE CELAYA

AV. 5 DE MAYO 39,

CENTRO HISTÓRICO

Founded in 1874 and decorated with antiques and a beautiful shop display, Dulcería de Celaya is one of the most famous sweet boutiques in Mexico City. The family-owned business still uses traditional techniques to make sweets from all over Mexico in their very own factory – it's pretty pricey but worth it!

BARRAS

1
LA OPERA CANTINA

AV. 5 DE MAYO 10, CENTRO HISTÓRICO

La Opera Cantina is the perfect spot to spend an evening tasting chiles en nogada, pulpo a la gallega or tacos de lechon and, of course, a pepino relleno! In reality, there are so many cantinas in Centro Histórico I could recommend, all with their own story to tell, special dish to try, music to listen to and drinks to enjoy, but the beauty of Opera Cantina will capture your heart!

2
SALÓN TENAMPA

PLAZA GARIBALDI 12, CENTRO, CUAUHTÉMOC

Tenampa bar is a traditional tequila and mariachi cantina right in Garibaldi and I guarantee that the fun atmosphere and music will entertain you for hours. They serve finger food platters, which are great when you want to try a bit of everything. The tequila menu is huge and the waiters are always happy to recommend something special.

3
LA COYOACANA

HIGUERA 14, LA CONCEPCIÓN, COYOACÁN

Make sure you book a table before heading to La Coyoacana as it's always busy, especially on weekends. They serve delicious specials during the week and the staff are super friendly. The awesome vibe is what makes this bar and grill one of the best in the area.

4
PULQUERÍA LA REFORMA DE LAS CARAMBOLAS

YERBABUENA 68, VICTORIA DE LAS DEMOCRACIAS, AZCAPOTZALCO

Pulque is a delicious beverage created from fermented agave and Pulquería La Reforma is the place to try it. The original drink comes from Hidalgo state, but the city has embraced it. Try the different flavours: pecan, guava, tomato, oyster and many more! The pulquería has been trading for more than 80 years, but the bar still consists of nothing more than a garage with a few plastic chairs and tables. Locals arrive early, and I recommend doing the same. Order a take-away pulque, choose your favourite flavour and sit back and enjoy the atmosphere!

5
CONEJO EN LA LUNA

CALLE ATLIXCO, CAMPECHE 132 ESQUINA, COLONIA CONDESA

This mezcal bar serves shots and cocktails at reasonable prices, along with a great atmosphere and live music. The molcajetes and tamales are delicious and the perfect accompaniment for the drinks!

6
RESTAURANTE ARROYO

AVENIDA INSURGENTES SUR 4403 SANTA ÚRSULA XITLA, TLALPAN

If you feel like going full on, then this bar and restaurant is for you, as it is the biggest Mexican restaurant in CDMX. They only serve traditional Mexican food and you can order literally whatever Mexican dish you want, from finger food to fine dining. They have a huge stage for live music and folklore dancers, and even a bullring.

ABOUT THE
AUTHOR

Rosa Cienfuegos is the owner of Sydney's much-loved Tamaleria and Mexican Deli that opened in 2017 and was the first tamaleria in Australia. Rosa started her business following the success of her Sydney market stall, as well as with encouragement from clients and friends who found a deep connection to her food. She has been named the Tamale Queen of Sydney, as well as a food ambassador by the Mexican community in Australia, for her dedication to opening paths for a new generation of Mexican restaurants, inspired by her approach to recreating the authentic cuisine of Mexico.

Rosa jumped at the opportunity to write her first cookbook, *Comida Mexicana*; her intention was always to introduce real Mexican food to the Australian community, and what better way than to share step-by-step recipes that show how easy and fun it is to cook authentic Mexican food at home, as well as the diversity of this glorious gastronomy! Writing a cookbook was the best way to get people excited to join the Mexican wave. After the release of *Comida Mexicana*, Rosa began cooking classes to teach everything from how to make tortillas to more complicated tamales, all mixed in with a bit of history, myth, traditions and, of course, cocktails to pair with the feast.

From home deliveries to food tours of Mexico, Rosa continues to grow her passion for this connection between Mexico and Sydney. She regularly travels to different parts of Australia to join food festivals, where she talks and empowers people to be creative and add a touch of Mexican ingredients to their pantries. She personally oversees the selection of ingredients and imported products from Mexico to her shelves, and frequently travels throughout her homeland to find the best suppliers, so her customers have exactly what they need for her recipes. For Rosa, working in hospitality is the best way to network and meet people interested in her culture, traditions and cooking methods, so don't be shy if you see her around, she is always happy to give advice on how to cook your favourite Mexican dish.

CDMX is Rosa's second cookbook, and it was made with the same love that she holds for her beloved Mexico City. It is surely not the last!

THANK YOU

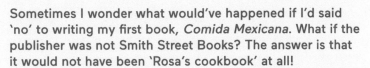

Sometimes I wonder what would've happened if I'd said 'no' to writing my first book, *Comida Mexicana*. What if the publisher was not Smith Street Books? The answer is that it would not have been 'Rosa's cookbook' at all!

I want to hugely thank the amazing team behind this book, for every email, every phone call, every due date, every photoshoot and every other little thing involved to make this dream come true. I do not have enough words to describe how blessed I am for having you hold my hand to make it as perfect as it is. Paul, Lucy, Alicia, Deb, Sarah, Caroline, Jane, Evi-O Studio – thank you. Working with you did not feel like working at all and I even feel like you knew me from when I was in Mexico! This cookbook is so ME and I love all your patience, time, dedication and help.

To my customers, friends and followers who support me and give me advice with kind words, phone calls, a shoulder to cry on and a coffee, beer or a hug whenever I feel down. To Carla, Graciela, Luis, Nancy, Juan Manuel, Stefan, Alan and so many more, thanks for being part of my journey and being my number-one fans! The love I feel from you is the best encouragement I need to keep it up and push myself to professionally grow and love what I do.

Special thanks to my dad, my best friend; my son, the motor of my life; my sister, my support; my nephew, my new little helper; my brother, my 'twin'; and my aunties Luz and Tere for every prayer you make for my wellbeing.

Finally, I would like to dedicate this book to my beautiful and incredible mother Carolina, who taught me to be tough and stubborn, and to never give up. Mamita linda, gracias for everything; even though we don't live in the same country, you are the most important female in my life and you have no idea how much I struggled writing this book knowing that you were facing a hard episode with treatments and pain. Life has been very generous, and second chances are definitely a gift. I love you with all my heart and I can't wait to spend more time with you close to me. Thank you for making me the strong, empowered and kind woman I am now.

I hope you feel the love in this book and its recipes as much as I enjoyed digging into my past to make it. GRACIAS!

Index

A

ACHIOTE 12
  Pulled-pork tostadas 58
Aguachile 168
Albondigas 143
Alitas de pollo 46
Apple salad 196
APRICOTS
  Chamoy salsa 222
  Cuban michelada 71
  Cucumber shots 74
  Dorilocos 70
Arroz de tres leches 200
Arroz Mexicano 237
Atun al chipotle 180
AVOCADOS 12
  Cheese tostadas 57
  Chilli prawns 168
  Guacamole 213
  mixed salad 182
  Salad for comida corrida 160
  Tampico-style steak 158

B

BACON
  Cheese-stuffed jalapenos 52
  Molletes with bacon 21
Baked chilli fish 174
Bean picaditas 51
Bean tostadas 54
BEANS 12
  Bean picaditas 51
  Bean tostadas 54
  Black bean gorditas 66
  Black beans 226
  Folded bean tortillas 150
  Ground beef tacos 98
  Molletes with bacon 21
  Pulled-pork tostadas 58
  Refried black beans 227
  Soy tostadas 63
  Tampico-style steak 158
  Tarasca soup 130
BEEF
  albondigas 143
  Corn in a cup with marrowbones 42

Ground beef tacos 98
Meatballs 143
'Old clothes' tacos 99
Shredded chilli beef tacos 104
Steak & cheese tacos 86
Steak in pasilla sauce with
  potatoes 149
Tampico-style steak 158
Tripe soup 118
Tripe tacos 90
BEER
  birria marinade 122
  Cuban michelada 71
  Goat soup 122
  Steak & cheese tacos 86
bell peppers:
  'Old clothes' tacos 99
Birria 122
birria marinade 122
Black bean gorditas 66
Black beans 226
Blistered jalapenos 238
Borrachitos 202
Bricklayers' eggs 35
'Burnt' flan 188

C

cacao 12
Cactus salad 161
cake, Sweetcorn 191
Caldo de camaron 179
Caldo de pollo 127
Camarones a la diabla 170
capsicum see bell peppers
Carne a la tampiquena 158
Carne en chile pasilla con papas 149
CARROTS
  Carrot salsa with habanero 220
  Chicken & vegetable soup 127
  Dorilocos 70
  Ground beef tacos 98
  Prawn soup 179
  Soy tostadas 63
celery: Chicken & vegetable soup 127
chamoy 12
Chamoy salsa 222
CHEESE 12
  Bean tostadas 54
  Cheese tostadas 57

Cheese-stuffed jalapenos 52
Cheesy prawn tacos 84
Chilaquiles with eggs 24
Chilli cheese corn pockets 64
Corn in a cup with marrowbones 42
Flour tortilla sandwiches 36
Folded bean tortillas 150
Mexican spaghetti 121
Molletes with bacon 21
Mushroom quesadillas 32
Steak & cheese tacos 86
Stuffed chillies 138
Tampico-style steak 158
Cheetos-dusted sweetcorn 43
CHICKEN
  Chicken & vegetable soup 127
  Chicken wings 46
  Green enchiladas 146
  Pork & hominy soup 123
  Shredded chilli chicken tacos 87
  Tampico-style steak 158
Chilaquiles con huevo 24
Chilaquiles with eggs 24
chile de árbol 13, 216
Chiles rellenos 138
CHILLIES 13
  Baked chilli fish 174
  Bean picaditas 51
  birria marinade 122
  Blistered jalapenos 238
  Bricklayers' eggs 35
  Cactus salad 161
  Carrot salsa with habanero 220
  Chamoy salsa 222
  Cheese tostadas 57
  Cheese-stuffed jalapenos 52
  Cheesy prawn tacos 84
  Chicken & vegetable soup 127
  Chicken wings 46
  Chilaquiles with eggs 24
  Chilli cheese corn pockets 64
  Chilli pork tacos 93
  Chilli prawns 168
  Chipotle tuna 180
  chorizo 108
  Cuban michelada 71
  Cucumber shots 74
  Devilled shrimp 170
  Dorilocos 70
  Fake guacamole 212
  Fish with garlic & chilli 173
  Fresh salsa 208

Fried tamales 22
Goat soup 122
Green enchiladas 146
Guacamole 213
Habanero salsa with mango 221
Meatballs 143
Mexican eggs 30
Mexican rice 237
Mexican spaghetti 121
Mushroom quesadillas 32
'Old clothes' tacos 99
Peanut & chile de árbol salsa 216
Peanut mole 157
Pork & hominy soup 123
Pork in green sauce 142
Potato & chorizo tacos 108
Potato & onion tacos 111
Prawn soup 179
Ranch eggs 18
Roasted green salsa 209
Seven chilli salsa 217
Shredded chilli beef tacos 104
Shredded chilli chicken tacos 87
Sliced chilli & cream tacos 103
Steak in pasilla sauce with potatoes 149
Steamed lamb pockets 94
Stuffed chillies 138
Tampico-style steak 158
Tarasca soup 130
Tortilla soup 116
Tripe soup 118
Chipotle tuna 180
chips, Tortilla 232
Chocolate tamales 195
chorizo 108
CORN 13
buying sweetcorn husks 22, 195
Cheetos-dusted sweetcorn 43
Chicken & vegetable soup 127
Corn in a cup with marrowbones 42
Ground beef tacos 98
masa 13
Sliced chilli & cream tacos 103
Soy tostadas 63
Sweetcorn cake 191
see also hominy
Corn tortillas 228
cream 13
Crispy tacos 151
Crumbled tortilla omelette 29
Cuban michelada 71
CUCUMBERS
Chilli prawns 168
Cucumber shots 74
Dorilocos 70
Salad for comida corrida 160

Devilled shrimp 170
Dorilocos 70

EGGS
Bricklayers' eggs 35
'Burnt' flan 188
Chilaquiles with eggs 24
Crumbled tortilla omelette 29
Mexican eggs 30
Ranch eggs 18
Sweetcorn cake 191
Elotes con cheetos 43
enchiladas, Green 146
Enchiladas verdes 146
Enfrijoladas 150
Ensalada de manzana 196
Ensalada de nopales 161
Ensalada para
comida corrida 160
EPAZOTE 13
Seven chilli salsa 217
Esquites con tuetano 42

Fake guacamole 212
FISH
Baked chilli fish 174
Chipotle tuna 180
Fish with garlic & chilli 173
Fried garlic fish 182
flan, 'Burnt' 188
Flour tortilla sandwiches 36
Flour tortillas 229
Folded bean tortillas 150
Food Lovers' Guide 241–6
Fresh salsa 208
Fried garlic fish 182
Fried tamales 22
Frijoles negros 226
Frijoles refritos 227

G

Goat soup 122
gorditas, Black bean 66
Gorditas de frijol 66
Gorditas de queso enchilado 64
Green enchiladas 146
Ground beef tacos 98
Guacamole 213
guacamole, Fake 212
Guacamole falso 212

H

Habanero salsa with mango 221
hibiscus flowers: Chamoy salsa 222
hominy: Pork & hominy soup 123
Horchata 78
Huevos a la Mexicana 30
Huevos al albanil 35
Huevos rancheros 18

J

Jalapenos rellenos de queso 52
Jalapenos toreados 238
jelly: 'Little drunks' 202
Jericallas 188

L

lamb: Steamed lamb pockets 94
LEMONS
Chicken wings 46
Habanero salsa with mango 221
LIMES 13
Blistered jalapenos 238
Chamoy salsa 222
Cheese tostadas 57
Chilli prawns 168
Corn in a cup with marrowbones 42
Cuban michelada 71
Cucumber shots 74
Dorilocos 70
Fake guacamole 212

Fresh salsa 208
Fried garlic fish 182
Guacamole 213
Paloma 77
Tampico-style steak 158
Tripe soup 118
Tripe tacos 90
'Little drunks' 202

M

MANGO
   Chicken wings 46
   Habanero salsa with mango 221
marinade, birria 122
masa 13
Meatballs 143
Mexican eggs 30
Mexican pantry 12–13
Mexican rice 237
Mexican spaghetti 121
Michelada Cubana 71
Migas con huevo 29
mixed salad 182
Mixiotes 94
Mojarras al mojo de ajo 182
Mole de cacahuate 157
mole, Peanut 157
Molletes con tocino 21
Molletes with bacon 21
Mushroom quesadillas 32

N

NOPALES 13
   Cactus salad 161

O

'Old clothes' tacos 99
omelette, Crumbled tortilla 29
ONIONS 13
   pickled red onion 58, 94
ORANGES
   Chamoy salsa 222
   Chicken wings 46

Habanero salsa with mango 221
Pulled-pork tostadas 58

P

Paloma 77
Pancita 118
pantry 12–13
PASTA
   Mexican spaghetti 121
   Pasta soup 132
Pastel de elote 191
PEANUTS
   Dorilocos 70
   Peanut & chile de árbol salsa 216
   Peanut mole 157
pecans: Apple salad 196
Pepinos rellenos 74
Pescado al ajillo 173
Pescado al horno en salsa de chiles 174
picaditas, Bean 51
Picaditas de frijol 51
pickled red onion 58, 94
Pico de gallo 208
pineapple: Apple salad 196
PLUMS 222
   Chamoy salsa 222
PORK
   Albondigas 143
   Chilli pork tacos 93
   Chocolate tamales 195
   chorizo 108
   Flour tortilla sandwiches 36
   Fried tamales 22
   Meatballs 143
   Peanut mole 157
   Pork & hominy soup 123
   Pork in green sauce 142
   Potato & chorizo tacos 108
   Pulled-pork tostadas 58
   Steak & cheese tacos 86
   see also bacon
POTATOES
   Baked chilli fish 174
   Chicken & vegetable soup 127
   Ground beef tacos 98
   Potato & chorizo tacos 108
   Potato & onion tacos 111
   Prawn soup 179
   Soy tostadas 63
   Steak in pasilla sauce with potatoes 149
Pozole rojo 123

PRAWNS
   Cheesy prawn tacos 84
   Chilli prawns 168
   Devilled shrimp 170
   Prawn soup 179
pudding, Rice 200
Puerco en salsa verde 142
Pulled-pork tostadas 58

Q

Quesadillas con hongos 32
quesadillas, Mushroom 32

R

Ranch eggs 18
Refried black beans 227
RICE
   Chicken & vegetable soup 127
   Horchata 78
   Mexican rice 237
   Rice pudding 200
Rice pudding 200
Roasted green salsa 209
rum: 'Little drunks' 202

S

SALADS
   Apple salad 196
   Cactus salad 161
   mixed salad 182
   Salad for comida corrida 160
Salsa chamoy 222
Salsa de cacahuate y chile de árbol 216
Salsa de habanero con mango 221
Salsa de siete chiles 217
Salsa de zanahoria con habanero 220
Salsa verde de chile asado 209
SALSAS
   Carrot salsa with habanero 220
   Chamoy salsa 222
   Fresh salsa 208
   Habanero salsa with mango 221
   Peanut & chile de árbol salsa 216

Roasted green salsa 209
Seven chilli salsa 217
tomato salsa 138
sandwiches, Flour tortilla 36
Seven chilli salsa 217
shots, Cucumber 74
Shredded chilli beef tacos 104
Shredded chilli chicken tacos 87
shrimp *see* prawns
Sincronizadas 36
Sliced chilli & cream tacos 103
Sopa aguada 132
Sopa de fideo seco 121
Sopa de tortilla 116
Sopa tarasca 130
SOUPS
    Chicken & vegetable soup 127
    Goat soup 122
    Pasta soup 132
    Pork & hominy soup 123
    Prawn soup 179
    Tarasca soup 130
    Tortilla soup 116
    Tripe soup 118
Soy tostadas 63
Steak & cheese tacos 86
Steak in pasilla sauce with
    potatoes 149
Steamed lamb pockets 94
Stuffed chillies 138
sweetcorn *see* corn
Sweetcorn cake 191
sweetcorn husks 22, 195

TACOS
    Cheesy prawn tacos 84
    Chilli pork tacos 93
    Crispy tacos 151
    Ground beef tacos 98
    'Old clothes' tacos 99
    Potato & chorizo tacos 108
    Potato & onion tacos 111
    Shredded chilli beef tacos 104
    Shredded chilli chicken tacos 87
    Sliced chilli & cream tacos 103
    Steak & cheese tacos 86
    Tripe tacos 90
Tacos de bistec con queso 86
Tacos de carne enchilada 93
Tacos de papas con cebolla 111
Tacos de papas con chorizo 108

Tacos de picadillo 98
Tacos de rajas con crema 103
Tacos de ropa vieja 99
Tacos de tinga de pollo 87
Tacos de tinga res 104
Tacos de tripa 90
Tacos dorados 151
Tacos gobernador 84
Tajin 13
tamarind: Chamoy salsa 222
TAMALES
    Chocolate tamales 195
    Fried tamales 22
Tamales de chocolate 195
Tamales fritos 22
Tampico-style steak 158
Tarasca soup 130
TEQUILA
    chorizo 108
    Cucumber shots 74
    Paloma 77
Textured Vegetable Protein (TVP): Soy
    tostadas 63
TOMATILLOS 13
    Albondigas 143
    Fake guacamole 212
    Green enchiladas 146
    Meatballs 143
    Pork in green sauce 142
    Tampico-style steak 158
TOMATOES
    birria marinade 122
    Bricklayers' eggs 35
    Cactus salad 161
    Cheese tostadas 57
    Cheesy prawn tacos 84
    Chicken & vegetable soup 127
    Chipotle tuna 180
    Devilled shrimp 170
    Fresh salsa 208
    Goat soup 122
    Ground beef tacos 98
    Guacamole 213
    Meatballs 143
    Mexican eggs 30
    Mexican rice 237
    Mexican spaghetti 121
    mixed salad 182
    'Old clothes' tacos 99
    Pasta soup 132
    Peanut mole 157
    Prawn soup 179
    Ranch eggs 18
    Refried black beans 227
    Salad for comida corrida 160
    Seven chilli salsa 217

Shredded chilli beef tacos 104
Shredded chilli chicken tacos 87
Soy tostadas 63
Stuffed chillies 138
Tampico-style steak 158
Tarasca soup 130
tomato salsa 138
Tortilla soup 116
Tripe soup 118
TORTILLA CHIPS 232
TORTILLAS
    Corn tortillas 228
    Flour tortillas 229
    Folded bean tortillas 150
Tortillas de harina 229
Tortillas de maiz 228
Tortilla soup 116
TOSTADAS
    Bean tostadas 54
    Cheese tostadas 57
    Pulled-pork tostadas 58
    Soy tostadas 63
    Tostadas 233
Tostadas de cochinita pibil 58
Tostadas de frijol 54
Tostadas de picadillo de soya 63
Tostadas de queso 57
Totopos 232
    Tripe soup 118
    Tripe tacos 90

Valentina sauce 13

wine: 'Old clothes' tacos 99

Z

zucchini: Fake guacamole 212

Smith Street Books

Published in 2023
by Smith Street Books
Naarm (Melbourne) | Australia
smithstreetbooks.com

ISBN: 978-1-9227-5458-5

Smith Street Books respectfully
acknowledges the Wurundjeri People
of the Kulin Nation, who are the
Traditional Owners of the land on which
we work, and we pay our respects
to their Elders past and present.

PUBLISHER
Paul McNally

PROJECT EDITOR
Lucy Heaver, Tusk Studio

NARRATIVE EDITOR
Jane Price

ART DIRECTION & DESIGN
Evi-O.Studio | Susan Le

PHOTOGRAPHER
Alicia Taylor

FOOD STYLIST
Deborah Kaloper

FOOD PREPARATION
Rosa Cienfuegos and Sarah Mayoh

TYPESETTER
Heather Menzies

PROOFREADER
Emily Preece-Morrison

INDEXER
Helena Holmgren

Printed & bound in China by C&C
Offset Printing Co., Ltd.

Book 285
10 9 8 7 6 5 4 3 2

MIX
Paper | Supporting
responsible forestry
FSC® C008047